LOVEMASTER'D
CRAIG SHOEMAKER

A DIGITAL JOURNEY TO LOVE AND HAPPINESS

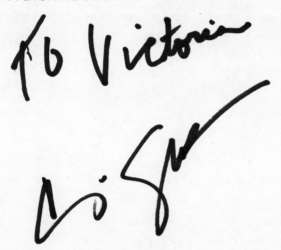

To Victoria

to Victor

"Drink deeply of the wealth of wisdom contained herein. It's the story of every man and woman alive. Told by a master storyteller, comedian, problem solver, and the guy, who cares profoundly about your relationships overcoming adversity and becoming relishable, delicious, and Omni- satisfying. The story is your story. As it effortlessly and irresistibly unfolds, your life will become the miracle, it was meant to be. Happy reading and re-reading. Be generous and share it with a friend in need."

— Mark Victor Hansen,
Co-Creator of the Chicken Soup for the Soul series

"From his comedic performances of the Love Master to Barney Fife you can tell Craig Shoemaker has an ear, but you also get the sense that the man listens. After reading this book you get just how well. LoveMaster'd is a beautiful read!"

— Whoopi Goldberg, Academy award winning actress

"Humorous and heart-wrenching, this is an epic sweep through the intense emotional, interpersonal, and legal odyssey of marital dissolution seen through the experience of two strangers clinging to one another as they navigate the stormy waters of families in trouble."

— Dr. Drew, Drew Pinsky, is an
American board-certified internist, addiction medicine
specialist, and radio and television personality

"20 years ago, trying to survive a marriage gone wrong, Craig Shoemaker's book would have been a perfect salve to my bruised soul and a beacon to keep moving toward during the humbling process of divorce. Now being happily in a relationship, the book serves as a reminder of the value of friendship and how sharing experiences, even the worst ones, brings meaning to our lives.

I will always have an extra copy of LoveMaster'd available to give to a friend when they are struggling in a relationship. The unguarded conversation between two friends trying to make sense of what did go wrong in their relationships is revealing and touching. I couldn't put it down. Sharing their stories with such generosity and humanity, the book is wonderfully cathartic for the reader and is going to help a lot of people."

— Jeanie Buss, President/Co-Owner,
Los Angeles Lakers. Author of "Laker Girl."

Produced by:

FriesenPress

Suite 300 – 852 Fort Street

Victoria, BC, Canada V8W 1H8

www.friesenpress.com

Distributed to the trade by The Ingram Book Company

Regarding the Sun...

*We can turn our heads toward the
Darkness, or look for the light.
It is our choice. We may stare
directly into the sun that blinds
us, or we can use it to light our path.
In the end, we cannot fully appreciate
the sun's warmth, until we've frozen
our asses off.*

– Craig Shoemaker

TABLE OF CONTENTS

FOREWORD

When I read a book, I many times either skim or ignore the forward. Don't do as I do. Read this! It sets up the whole thing and this "thing" is outside the norm. This ain't your daddy's self-help book!

I'm a standup comedian and have been paid to be one for over thirty years. To make a living as a comic, calls for an ability to have a good sense of general vibration about people. An ardently developed sense of compassion, empathy, and awareness has been essential in sustaining a successful career. Comedy boiled down to its simplest form is an identification of truth, so the closer I am to being authentic (even when exaggerated for comedic effect), the heartier the laughs.

The soulful relationship with an audience, whether it is in a filled theatre or one-on-one, propels me through life. The more I focus on peeling away and discarding the layers that prevent honest connection of self or others, the better the outcome. These skills that have helped me become a successful standup have been essential to my journey. As a dedicated husband and father, the definition of purpose and passion to self-actualize has been of prime importance to my children's well being too. The more I grow and transform, the more my family benefits from it.

To move into a space of gratitude and happiness was not an easy transition. I was not bequeathed money, property, good values in the love department, or formal education; so I learned early on to push though any conditions with enormous self-will and strong resolve.

I was parented by absent, unstable and battling parents, which is a tall order, and it has been a plodding and painful path. The search for maternal and paternal figures took me to dark and scary places. I become a rebellious student and juvenile delinquent, often waking up in a drug, sex, or alcohol-induced fog, wondering where I was or if what was next to me was human.

Fortunately, the expedition eventually led me to the most extraordinary, happy, and love-filled life I ever could have imagined. Today, I am passionately in love with my wife and children and I cannot express enough how grateful I am to all that is present in my life today.

Although an experienced, twenty-five-year member of the Writer's Guild of America, I could never have constructed a life story this beautiful and magnificent if you gave me an unlimited supply of pen and paper, and a decade in a secluded cabin. I am blessed to have had the trials and difficulties of the past, for without the high walls to climb; I would not be able to fully appreciate the daily reprieve I enjoy now. There have been numerous rewards and awards from television, film and radio, but nothing compares to the infinite supply of happiness/serenity trophies I have today. A Bachelor's degree and a Doctorate degree signify a determination and dedication to learning. Looking at our family home, it appears that the most essential school of higher learning is an elevated soul.

That is not to say that the pilgrimage is over or I am anywhere near complete. Far from it. However, I now tread upon a path of inspired optimism and great peace on a regular basis. For a panic-stricken, confused kid; this is a miracle!

For the past five years, I have been utilizing Facebook as a place to conduct business, as well as initiate conversation. Two years ago, I came across a message in my personal Facebook inbox from a woman I'd known from afar for some years. Her name was Leah. At the time, she was married to a guy named Matt, whom I had met with her at a handful of my comedy shows when I traveled back to my hometown Philly area. Even though I am kind-of known in some circles as a "celebrity," Leah opened up a little bit to simply inform me that she and Matt were divorcing after almost thirty years of marriage. I was soon to find out that Leah wanted to share her story with me because she felt a kinship and connection through our prior Facebook posts.

Something powerful within my soul nudged me delve deeper with Leah than she may have intended me to go, and I was inclined to assist her in what she was about to go through.

What unfolded was an unconventional, uncommon, unfiltered and undeniably powerful exchange between two adults on the mend. Our 200 plus-page heart-to-heart was an amazing healing for both of us.

This book is a private-message Facebook dialogue between two people in the midst of tremendous change, subsequent pain, and eventual heart restoration. By identifying our own struggles, it became easy for us to see that these are the same obstacles countless folks go through on a regular

CRAIG SHOEMAKER

basis. By witnessing what it took to get to the other side of adversity, we gave one another hope...especially during the times when we couldn't see a light in our own present conditions.

Leah and I have agreed that sharing our story through this method has the potential to help many others. We have changed names for certain people's protection, and let's say that "some" of the stories may be fabricated. What is fact and what is fiction is irrelevant, because it is all rooted in universal truth.

This book documents our unique journey through life's storms; not so dissimilar to Dorothy's from *The Wizard of Oz*. Our walk through fear and seemingly insurmountable odds is very real and profound. It is our wish that this book give hope to the hopeless and inspiration to the uninspired. After all, every storm eventually comes to an end...some even end with rainbows.

—Dr. Craig Shoemaker

CHAPTER ONE

"I AM THAT, I AM"

Leah De Luca   1/13, 5:06pm

Hi Craig! Listen, since I thought we might see you after your next show, I should probably let you know that Matt and I are splitting up after 30 years of marriage. You've hung out with us a few times and we share some things in common, so I thought I would let you in on this. From meeting you after shows and from what I see from your life on Facebook, you seem like a compassionate man, and I figured you would understand. It's all very sad and extremely difficult. I never fully appreciated what others who were divorcing were really going through. It's hard on everyone, including our two daughters and two sons. That said, in my heart, I know I did all I could to make it work and I know it's for the best. Keep us in your thoughts. I still love reading your posts because they make me smile. I need that these days. Hope all is well with you and your beautiful family.

Craig Shoemaker   1/14, 9:26am

So sorry you are going through this. Indeed, it is a difficult, stressful and heart breaking time, but if you get through this with as much grace and integrity as you can muster up, peace and blissfulness will be yours. I am amazed with the results, once I made the decision to be as loving and patient as possible – even if that was the last thing in the room.

I read many of your posts and know you are a beautiful human being with an amazing spirit. Whatever happens in this process will be okay. I cannot believe how my life unfolded after I made some clear decisions about what I TRULY wanted. Everyone around me, including my ex-wife, now benefits from my choice of grounding in goodness, kindness and higher consciousness. I can feel your vibration all the way over here 3000 miles away in sunny Southern California. Know that you have a wonderful and full life at your fingertips. Matt will be a perfect teacher for you. You might carry out the divorce or you may find that you love him more and become closer. Results will manifest in a great way if you stay on the road you are on. Much love and happiness, whatever path you choose!

Leah De Luca   1/14, 7:04pm

Wow! Your kind and thoughtful words inspire me, Craig.
Thanks so much for the note. I am going to hold onto and
refer to it every now and then when I need a little lift or a
reminder of what is good on this earth. God Bless.

Craig Shoemaker   1/15, 2:29pm

I connect with your words, even if they just appear on
someone else's FB wall. You are very special. Obviously, I do
not know you that well. I don't know Matt that well either, but
it does not matter when it comes to concerns of this nature.
My heart is phoning and I'm not declining this call.

To be honest, I have had a robust urge to assist others in
finding alternative ways to heal and find happiness for quite
some time now. It appears as if my life-pain endurance test
is something to let people in on, yet, I am many times too
afraid of those who give off that condemning, judgmental
pulse. A lot of work went into developing new patterns and
this repetition brought me to fresh instincts; an impulse that
is now instructing me to go beyond normal bounds.

Let me start by saying that the last seven years of dealing
with my divorce have delivered some of the most gut wrench-
ing, demoralizing, depressing and hopeless days of my life.
It took our family into a space that almost destroyed us all
– emotionally, financially and spiritually.

Yet, my ex-wife became the ultimate tutorial for me, like going
to spiritual grad school. I flunked many tests along the way
and still get an occasional "C-minus." Through deepened
faith and committed work on my insides, magnificence has
finally been revealed and realized. I have to laugh because
my ex always insults me and warns that our sons "will eventually know what kind of father you are," as she claims I am
an abusive bully. But this time she was right about one thing
– Michael and Johnny now DO know who Daddy is, and this
is a very GOOD thing!

It took simple acts, composure and then learning how to get
out of my own habits, turning my wish for things to go "my
way" over to a higher source. Just like Dorothy in *The Wizard
of Oz,* I learned that I had the answers all along. I just had to

go on a long and difficult journey to reach my ultimate home, my good heart & soul.

Forgiveness, sacrificing ego and gratitude are key principles I must stay close to. It takes a whole lot of time digging holes to find the whole. I hope you can remember this when things seem bleak. At times, the light appeared to be extinguished but now it shines brighter than ever.

I've made millions of people laugh for decades, which leaves me wondering why some measureless force would lead me through such extended anguish. I want to write a book called, *God's a Slow Mother Fucka!* How dare he make me suffer and take his good ole time showing me happiness?

My ex's speed dial on my old Blackberry was an "F" which stood for "fuckin' asshole." Over the years, I pressed it with such ferocious resentment that I practically wore out the letter on my dial pad. Yet eventually, I chose to gently press it with a smile, changing the "F" word to "Forgiveness," thus revising the entire energy. Now I look at my ex as a child who strays off the sidewalk so I give her light, which results in a lightening up of something that had an illusion of frightening darkness.

Sorry if I rambled a bit. Just wanted to throw out some words to you, in case you might be going through some tough times. I have such empathy for you and anyone going through tumultuous times. Much love to you & Matt.

 Leah De Luca   1/16, 7:09pm

Thank you Craig. Your journey clearly has not been an easy one. But it has made you the man you are. I know I don't know you that well but I also feel I can share some of my story with you. I hope you don't see this as trying to throw Matt under the bus. I wouldn't have built a life with him if I didn't know and experience the good in him. That said, I have also endured some painful experiences. While it's tempting to want to direct "blame" at Matt solely for the behavior, deep down I reflect upon what my role has been in the things that have happened.

I am not one who likes failure and I will not get "stuck" in the past but I hope to learn and grow from it. Some of Matt's acting out in varying forms has been going on for so long that I have long since forgiven him. But as the cycle of hurt repeated itself, it also slowly eroded our relationship. For years I've been looking in the mirror, almost not recognizing who I was any more, wondering who "Matt & Leah" had become as a couple.

We put on a good show. At least I did, covering things up from family, friends and our kids. I became an expert at it, or so I thought. Upholding the "Matt & Leah Show" became a full time job for me. At any rate, I lost a lot of self-respect in staying with someone who I allowed to treat me very badly much of the time. When Matt finally realized that I couldn't go on living that way, he articulated his sorrow and made promises to change, as he has repeatedly done many times before. Only this time, I couldn't go on with the pattern any more.

Now, only a few months later, I am stunned at the 180-degree turnaround. His pleas of sorrow and expressions of undying love have turned to what feels like pure hatred directed towards me. It is so hurtful and I am incredulous to some extent. I ask myself, "How can someone I've been married to for so long have such hatred for me now?" What did I do? I wonder whether any of it was real. I have expressed my deep desire to have some type of relationship with Matt going forward, if for nothing else than for our amazing children. He wants no part of that. Yet, in spite of so many dark things that have happened, I actually still care deeply for Matt. I always will. My hope for him is that he finds greater meaning in his life and happiness, because everyone deserves to be happy.

I have not opened up to many, other than my immediate family and very dearest friends, so thanks for listening. Talking with someone who can be objective and has been through it really helps. I still have a long journey of healing ahead and I would appreciate knowing about any of the tools you used to get to the place you are now. I will get there, and when I do, I hope that I too, can help others.

 Craig Shoemaker   1/16, 11:41pm

I don't regard anything you say as throwing Matt under the bus, just as I'm sure anything I say, you would not consider a betrayal to him. You are not betraying Matt by getting well. Contrarily, if you take certain bold steps it will ultimately HELP him. What is most important is that there is a mutual understanding that we are all flawed humans trying to make sense of things, live well and get past certain hurts.

Right now, you are transitioning into freedom. Through my own process, I found that the way to reach higher ground is to let go of fears, secrets and outmoded thoughts that imprisoned me for so long. Honesty and readiness are the first moves toward finding peace within, and hence, within others.

I dig what you say about blame. It's just the truth. We all blame, especially when we appear to be attacked without provocation. When she once again accuses me like a criminal on a witness stand, I profess my "innocence" to my ex-wife on countless occasions. I still do. It never works to assuage her anger. Most of the time, my defensiveness actually heightens her commitment to attack.

I have to be honest, most days I still can't stand Debby. I cannot believe I was ever married to this woman. Yet, I look at the dynamic I created and know she was part of what I needed on my expedition to discover my true self. Without her, there'd be no Michael, no Johnny or even Jackson, who I have with my wife Mika; the sum total of love in my life. Without an insane ex-wife, I would not have passed the test that has led me to the discovery of unconditional love.

I try not to beat myself up for the ill feelings I have about Debby. These feelings are real and to deny them would be huge disservice to my growth. Phoniness only takes me backwards. For many years, I bought into this whole "image" thing, "looking good" for others being of prime importance. I pretended, turning my head away from reality, in favor of living in denial. I showed the outside world, whether it be with peers or a comedy audience, a life that was not real......*I made others happy when I was dying inside*.

You know what that is? LYING. I lived a lie in my marriage to Debby; a lie of omission and lack of authenticity. I loved the IDEA of her, but not the real her. In that marriage, I became a person who was not ME. Once I recognized my own deception, the road to reclamation became more manageable and promising.

You're MUCH further along than I was when I began my divorce 7 years ago. I'm amazed at what you write and how you're so self aware about not being a victim, resulting in searching within for the answers. But we fall on our faces many times. That's okay. Sounding like a victim or feeling crappy is necessary for growth.

I've been a rescuer/people-pleaser for a very long time. When I finally reached my lowest point, it took a clear decision to change. Many who knew me were uncomfortable with the revisions. They didn't like the turnaround, since they were very comfy being the recipient of my agenda to get them to love me by helping them. I now pick self-fulfillment over their need to be taken care of and it pisses 'em off. Let me tell you, babies let out a scream when you cut the umbilical cord and for many it has been deafening.

Some friends and family deemed me to be selfish when I told them I was getting divorced. Maybe they were in fear, or perhaps they wished they had the courage to create a remodel for themselves. As the constant "tests" were delivered daily, I realized that I needed to be "fit" to cope with the difficulties thrust upon me. It's similar to training for a boxing match. Proper mental and physical conditioning prepares me for all that comes at me.

However, centeredness in a divine source was the essential last station of the workout regimen. Through this process, I found that the more "spiritually fit" I am, the more equipped I am to handle any situation. It takes daily practice and discipline. If I don't do what it takes, I step off the path of enlightenment and good will. What I want you to know is that you are not alone. Perhaps you can relate to what I am saying. Ask me anything or share whatever you need... *the truth shall set us free*!

Reminds me, I gotta go do a few sets of Serenity Squats. ;)

 Leah De Luca   1/17, 5:00am

Your words resonate with me. Reading them helps me see some things I really still need to work on with myself, especially the spiritual aspect, which I now see was key for you on the road to healing and divine happiness. I need to search within for spiritual growth and healing, I am lacking there.

Also, one thing that again jumps off the page to me is your comment that you "loved an IDEA of her, but not the real her." I have actually used these same words in reconciling the conflicting feelings I have while on this emotional roller coaster. One feeling I don't have for Matt is hatred. I often hate what he does (or what he did), but I don't hate him. I can't hate him. Some people close to me who know about the things that have happened during our time together find this hard to believe. They are almost frustrated that I am not angrier with him.

I spent many years hiding our problems. I became numb to the lunacy of it all. Over time, I began to believe that my life with Matt was "normal," when it was anything but that. The only anger I have at this stage is the way he is handling himself during this divorce process, particularly regarding the things he wants from me. As I write this, I guess I should recognize this is the victim part of me revealing itself. I feel like; "Are you kidding me? After all the pain you inflicted on me and now I have to PAY you for it too?" I can't tell you how much I want to let go of these feelings. This is what drives some of my fears about having finally taken this big step. As you say, I have to look at things differently and let go of the ideas and fears. I want to scream, "I don't care if I walk away with nothing as long as I find a way to peace!" But, I'm not there yet, although I am working on it.

Anyway, one of the biggest feelings I wrestle with now is deep sadness. Sadness for what feels like giving up on the family I always wanted and seeing it fall apart. Matt and I are the first in both of our immediate families to divorce. Sadness for the "IDEA" of the Matt I wanted. Sadness for my kids. Friends and loved ones say, "They'll be fine. You raised them well and they are young adults." Yet I know they are hurting, embarrassed, and feel cheated. Cheated from being part of a "whole" and traditional family unit – they deserve that. Sadness over the feelings of loss of my in-laws, who I love. I hope when this is over I will reconnect with them on some level but it will never be the same. Sadness over missing Matt. Yes, that's right, I miss him. But again, I miss the idea and not the reality.

It's funny the things you hear from people when going through a divorce. People mean well. Over and over, I hear things like, "You have so much to offer. You are intelligent, beautiful, have a great career, you're a good person, you will find someone who really loves you like you deserve." I don't know if this is normal but I have to tell you that looking for someone else, or hoping someone finds me, is honestly the last thing on my mind. Like you before Mika, I don't think I have ever had true, unconditional love in a partner and yes, I'd love to find that. But I have to find the "true me" first. That's my little project. My one-woman show in the making.

 Craig Shoemaker   1/17, 9:12am

(In Yoda's voice) "Yes, young Padawan, well on your way to grasping truth, you are." Just so you know, I can pretty much surmise some of what happened with Matt. Feel free to let me hear anything you believe will assist you in breaking loose from the ties that currently bind you. In my case, it was so hard to reveal specific things but the truth does indeed untie the knots that bind us. Please know I don't think what you write is done to "out" Matt. I don't hear it as blame or victimhood. I get it. I won't judge Matt either, for whatever you say does not represent his entire being, or the entire story does not represent his entire being, or the entire story, but is merely a reflection of a man who might have lost his way.

Regarding my own marriage to my ex, after many years of couple's therapy of varying styles, direction and counselors, I finally had enough. Usually a hopeful guy, I saw no hope. I mustered up the courage to move out and on. My mantra was, "There has got to be something better for me out there and in here," (pointing to a broken heart). The negation of a truth system I had built through a lifetime started to chip away. To have a knowing that there is so much more outside the box I was placed into became so exciting to me. I had acted the part for the script I was handed, and now it was time to live the magnificent story I deserved!

When I made these bold steps, the "bully" part of Debby was challenged. See, she was raised to get her own way no matter what, and now she was going to war with her perceived betrayer – me. I married a pretty woman, but forgot that many people who have always been beautiful on the outside, don't tend to develop other qualities, since so many parents and others "spoil" good-looking girls and boys. A narcissist expects, and when it is not given, you are beheaded by the queen.

Nothing I did appeased her. It was ON and no weapon was spared! Power and control are such destructive forces when endorsed and emboldened by fear and anger. Fear leads to awful events but in our society, we are not taught to deal with it in a mature and healthy way. We ignore it, pretending it doesn't exist. As men, we are instructed to march on with strength. We hear the messages: "Do not show weakness, never give in, and never quit until you have annihilated your opponent!" Remember this Leah; the anger that is directed at you is not related to you, but is about the personal demons that he can't reckon with in his quest to win.

I tried so incredibly hard to be civil and reasonable with Debby but it takes two willing parties for that to take place. It seemed like no matter which road I took, the results were fruitless and even more damage took place. At first, we went to a mediator and didn't retain a lawyer. We got nowhere. One day, Debby was actually bodily removed by the mediator, as she stormed in through the door, after already being put in a separate room. I began to think that no amount of compromise was enough and no amount of sacrifice would ever be sufficient. Now that I look back, of course that was the case!

Debby and I had spent years within dysfunctional marriage conditions, so why would it change during divorce proceedings? She's the meanest fighter I have ever known. I used to call her "Jerry Quarry," after the Irish brawler who fought Muhammad Ali. Yet somehow, during mediation, I expected her to put down the gloves and be LOVING?? It's similar to warriors, trained to kill and defeat the delegated foe, and then when peace is declared, they have no clue how to proceed.

I lived much of my life believing the notion that power and control is the definition of winning. It certainly is not. That's the illusion we buy into from birth. Actually, my losses have delivered the greatest victories I have ever achieved, and this comes from a man with a lifetime of supposed "achievements" on stage and screen. What I gained from letting go of old, thrust-upon concepts is infinite, beautiful and enduring. Without question, it's a new world of possibility, far from the dark acceptance of mediocrity that I was raised to believe I deserved.

Finally, after many months of stress and fighting for things previously foreign to me, my ex-wife and I, alas, did reach an agreement. This lasted longer than a gnat takin' a leak. It quickly became revealed that Debby needed my blood, since I was the one allegedly causing her such pain.

Her agenda for revenge took an unexpected and horrid turn. When we were together, I often told her I could write a book about her called, *How Low Will She Go?* – for it seemed she would do virtually anything to take me out. If she told the truth, it would be by accident. Well, I guess I shouldn't have put that thought out to the universe, for she went WAY past any idea I had about low. Soon after our separation, even as we were signing an agreement, she secretly and maliciously had me reported to Child Services for supposedly molesting both our sons.

... and it became the most devastating, puzzling, inexplicable, trying and depressing days of my life.

All of what I thought was true was now challenged to a degree I had never known. Although I was 100 percent innocent, this does little good when someone makes these charges. Just as she has done her entire life, she escalated the drama for all involved, including the family courts, thus pulling focus from Debby's personal demons. There was no skirting around issues for me this time. Only diligent honesty and absolute removal of negativity (by me) would transform this situation. So began a dizzying, perplexing and tumultuous ride with the ex; just the way she likes it. She's the Carny Coaster operator on meth. Eventually the machine will stop but not until she says it will. Your hair is frayed, heart is racing and nerves are on red alert. You undo your safety harness and walk past her to: "Have a nice day." It's another day at the fair for people of this ilk. To this day, I wonder if she is aware of how much she lies and fabricates, or whether her mental illness prevents her from ever knowing? It has been proven time and time again, at the cost of all of our family's savings, that I am innocent of all the fabricated assertions Debby has made. I took polygraphs and submitted to any and all evaluations. I retained "witnesses" to my alleged abuse to minors by dipping into money I don't have, to hire a nanny.

Nothing works. Her allegations are her "go-to" when she feels threatened. For instance, a lawyer asked her to compromise on something, and she spits back, "Craig is molesting my boys!" Guess what? No human being is going to ignore this kind of a claim. It is natural for folks to protect children. This mother uses this fact to try to gain advantage, no matter how much it is proven not to be fact. We have never completed a trial and so forth, only going back every so often to deal with her latest accusations. She keeps thinking, like I did

CRAIG SHOEMAKER

and so many others she sets up for the con, that she will be "rescued" by a court of law. The thought and threat is always there with her, even if a hundred people told her to move on. Once the court told us they were done with this crap, it still didn't make her switch it up. Debby just puts the judge on the list of those who are out to get her.

Even our oldest son tries to tell her it is all lies. She yells back at him that he's messing with her reality, or claims I am coaching him. Yes, it is real to her…I think. Perception is quite the law in her world.

I'm still not sure of the mechanics behind a person who acts in this way of absolute righteous attack. One thing I must let go of is trying to figure too much of it out. It is what it is, no matter what the diagnosis or cause.

Every time I reacted to her incessant, accusatory pop quizzes, I fell deeper down the rabbit hole. I thought to myself, *What she did is the most heinous, despicable thing a person could do!* So I figured any angry response on my part was justified. Strangely, I ended up mirroring the pathology that I sought to escape, as I too wanted to be "right" at all costs. I began to fight dirty. When I reverted to these old, bad tactics, I hopped off the path of goodness and kindness and jumped on the ugly bandwagon of revenge and resentment. I got nasty. I got loud. I searched for people to tell me I was right. I gossiped and assassinated her character, thinking that she deserved it, and that my crime of bad rumors paled in comparison to what she said to anyone within earshot.

Although I first thought I could manage the difficult circumstances myself, as I had since I was a child, I finally hired an attorney and supplied the information that I figured would assist the legal team in taking my opponent down. In the end though, I became my own worst enemy. Ugliness ensued and my suffering became incomprehensible.

One thing I always kept in mind was the welfare of our children. I kept thinking about how I was the captain of their ship and they were the passengers. This divorce was like the perfect shit storm and it was my job as their father, a skilled veteran of the seas, to find the best way to negotiate through any conditions and to do so with peaceful grace and confident ease. Did my passengers, especially being young children, care about my feelings about who or what "started" the storm? Would they benefit from my rage about the conditions of the weather? A rocky ocean cannot change an ultimate course. All climate conditions are temporary, but our destination is infinite. As their captain, it was my duty to ensure that my tiny travelers trusted me. Love, tolerance and inspiration serve them better than indignation and blind anger. As their father, I *had no choice* but to hold steady with the absolute knowing that all will be okay in the end.

Initially, the courts took their mother's side, which put me deeper into my trip through hell. I get it now (but not then) that the authorities must take the safe way and assume the mother's story is correct. They are obligated to protect children at all costs. Leah, those days were bleak, to say the least. It saddens me deeply to even write about it, knowing that this is still going on, albeit to a lesser degree, with Debby pulling stunts when least expected.

I hate what the ugliness of divorce has done to our family and yet, I can't ignore the fact that this torrential tsunami delivered me onto peaceful shores I could have never known if not for this endurance test. Now, I have a better appreciation and understanding of what it takes to get to Nirvana. I slip whenever I resort to old, retributive behavior but I now have the skills to return to a space of internal richness. Through the trails of this journey, I have come to know two acronyms that helped me immensely:

#1. EGO is "Edging God Out"
#2. FEAR is "False Evidence APPEARING Real"

Okay, family is up, so I gotta run. To be continued....

Leah De Luca   1/18, 5:48am

I will respond tonight. Let me say for now, that it's difficult to wrap my head around what you must've gone through, Craig. Then again, seeing how you are fulfilled and thriving today, is just unbelievable. I know I have much to learn from you and your experiences. I really appreciate your friendship and hope it's not one where I just "take," but have something to give, despite the insanity that is my life at this moment. Back soon!

Craig Shoemaker   1/18, 7:29pm

Leah, I "slipped" today. Dealing with old, toxic relationship patterns is literally like recovering from drug addiction. If I don't do what is necessary for my recovery, I resort to negative, old behavior. I woke up at 2:30 am, unable to get back to sleep until 5 am, then woke up when my kids came into the bedroom at 7 to get me. I was rushed and drove like a bat out of hell to get them to school on time.

See where this one's going? I was not centered and at peace to begin my morning. I grew more restless throughout the day. I did not execute the quiet maintenance that it takes to ground myself, instead, I put energy into the verbal tennis matches going on my head, volleying back and forth about what I would say to my ex in an attempt to show her the way. Ha! As if!

I tried to come up with the words that would make her change and actually began to think I could form sentences that would make her see the error of her ways. Surely, this time my ex would listen and heed my advice, right? I raised my voice and became obstinate and belligerent. This is not the man I am or intend on being. I feel as if I am walking backwards. I see nothing but darkness, all due to not starting my day bathing in light. Everything I hate about her, I loathe in myself. She is like a giant funhouse mirror, reflecting my image in twisted distortion. I clearly see every defect in her, so as to ignore the exact deficiency in Craig that begs attention. Unreasonable expectations beget harm in what would otherwise be harmony. When I make my raison d'être about curing her or anybody else, I suffer and so does my family around me. I am aware that my negative stuff pales in comparison to hers but that acknowledgement serves no objective, giving rise to the illusion that there is a "score," and I am the keeper. Ironically (or not), I hate scorekeepers.

Just wanted to let you in on the spiritual diversion. Writing to you puts me back where I need to be. I hope this assists you as well.

Leah De Luca   1/19, 8:48pm

Hey Craig. I have tried for two nights to respond and found myself falling into the trap of writing a diatribe about Matt and my present circumstances...and then deleted...re-wrote and deleted again. Suffice it to say that stress takes a toll on the physical body. I have felt betrayed and abused in some ways, during my marriage to Matt. Am I so arrogant that I would say I had nothing to do with any of this? No. I haven't really come to grips with what my role was in all that happened but I know I have had some role. Reflecting on this, without blaming myself, is part of the process and part of the healing for me.

The amazing thing is that the day when you wrote to me about the darkness you went through was one of my darkest days yet. We are still at the beginning stages of divorce; claim and counterclaim filed, case statements being prepared. You know how it goes. But things have been awful at home over the last few months as we have been living in the same house. I'm not sure where he is now. He disappears, comes and goes to get mail, and no longer communicates. I only know he has been around when the mail is mysteriously gone when I get home from work.

At any rate, I received a letter from his attorney two days ago; full of twisted versions of the truth, and several lies and attacks. Could it be? I had just read your story about the "bully" in your ex-wife. To have lies told about you...and then to see it writing...well, it's really something. Why does it feel even worse when lies are in writing? One such lie was that I threatened to go to the police and falsely accuse him of domestic violence. Really? Did I threaten to call the police? Yes, but never to falsely accuse anyone of anything.

My initial reaction was to want to go on the offensive and call my attorney after reading this letter; falling into that trap. Thankfully, my lawyer is a great guy and talked me off that ledge. My response will be limited to setting the record straight. I am not taking the bait and that is in large part because of what you have shared with me. I also trust that the truth sets us free. Although, that doesn't alleviate the pain of this process and it doesn't lessen the blow when you think, or rather, hope that people will be honest and ethical. This whole thing sucks, plain and simple.

Please keep sharing if you are so inclined. To know that you have setbacks, in spite of the tremendous progress, just demonstrates your honesty and that you are real. It helps me set realistic expectations for myself in this process. Oh, one other thing. I think I honestly knew before I married Matt, that this marriage might be a mistake. Feels healing to admit that. That said, I wouldn't trade it for anything, because I could not imagine my life without the joy I have had in being a mother to my kids. Yes, I could have had kids otherwise, but not these four. I feel very blessed, despite my present circumstances!

Craig Shoemaker 1/20, 12:13am

Yesterday, I reconnected with a brother on this planet whom I haven't seen in a while. His name is Mikki, and he is one of the greatest men of integrity and high values I've ever met. Our talk lasted for hours, and this will sound strange, but I felt like I levitated at one point – my entire body and soul suddenly filled up with such monumental positive emotion that I had an out-of-body (but in-body) moment. It felt as if my chair lifted off the ground as we sat in a restaurant exchanging intentions and ideas as to what we want to bring to the planet. It makes me laugh sometimes when I think of the "Dungeon Gang" I was in during high school, where we were lifted to new dimensions by other "methods." After that came a fraternity, with the entire mission being to get wasted as much as possible. I can't believe I survived my past but am sure glad I did, so I can immerse myself in the wonder that exists in the now.

Seeing Mikki, who recently had a personal transformation of tremendous magnitude, reminded me of a movie he made that I wanted to turn you onto. It's called *The Moses Code,* and is the story of the code of Moses, broken down into the simplest of terms. Perhaps you have heard that the name God as written in the Old Testament, Yahweh, translates to "I am that I am." Yet the secret lies within a punctuation mark. Specifically, it's a comma. If you put a comma after "that," you have the true meaning of the passage, "I am that, I am."

This message remains loud and clear for me. What it says is that all living things on this earth are connected. We are all one and if I look at all people, whether friend or foe, I will see myself in them. I am them and they are me; infinite souls sharing the human experience. I've actually walked around trying this on for size and it is a lot of fun, as this wisdom creates an empathic response in me. I now know that all I love or detest is contained within myself. Obviously, I don't like my ex-wife's actions or way of being, yet my emotional response is merely the reflection of the parts of me I'd like to evolve.

Many times I'll see somebody acting boorish or brash and think, *How can they do that and live with themselves?* In retrospect, and upon closer inspection, I find that I'm actually jealous of these people. HOW, you might say? For example; what if someone says what he or she wants, but does so loud and obnoxiously? What if they express themselves like this on a regular basis? They are doing what I wish I would do - taking care of their needs! If they keep getting their way, even through being bullish or a squeaky wheel, I resent it because I actually want my way, yet feel powerless in my attempt to secure my needs, internalizing what I desire so as not to rock a boat.

I am that, I am...

I observe someone express how they feel, even if it's really ugly, while I sit there silent and worried what people will think of me. Strangely, I work so hard at making others believe I am not self-involved that I forget how to self-love. My temper has flared at times. This is not the sum total of who I am, but is a part of me that goes mostly unexpressed. And the same goes for my ex-spouse. She is not all evil, even if I think that to be the case when I witness pure hatred. This is the part of her that gets magnified when I resent raising children with a partner who deplores me.

I am that, I am...

Perception is a large part of the battle. If I am grounded in goodness and spirit, I can see the glow within her. If I look at the world while steeped in resentment, I encounter gloom. The more I embrace myself devoid of judgment, the more compassion I find myself having for her. She is my GREATEST professor, bringing the lessons to my heart and soul, as I deepen my understanding of my life's meaning. I look back and laugh at some of our insane fights, where each of us is trying so hard to be right, both jockeying for the rights to moral high ground. We lowlight the other's offenses, as if this absolves one another from our own attacks. Each of us taking turns calling the cops, as if to show the world just who was to blame for the mess, all the while forgetting there are children bearing witness to this insidious conduct.

CRAIG SHOEMAKER

I married my ex-wife for reasons like yours. I tried to do everything I could to make her happy. My immaturity had me embracing the thought that if I could only make my wife happy, all would be good. I literally married my mother. With both my mom and Debby, through their occasional acknowledgment or light praise, I felt good for a moment and called that "love." They gave me crumbs and I made a cake out of them. I acted like it was a big, delicious dessert and feigned extreme pleasure to even my closest friends. To this day, my mom cannot utter the words "I love you" to me. Sorrow pours over me as I mourn the missed opportunity of experiencing a "mother's love." When I read court documents from my former spouse, in which she uses my mom and sister as supporters in her "cause," it is truly devastating.

I many times live within a giant ball of denial. I still do when I hold hope that my mother will come around and see me for the whole person I am, not for the fragment of what she conceives me to be. I know who I am today and am actually proud of the being that is me. Not of achievements or accomplishments, but the person *that, I am*. We are all a work in progress, and I sincerely wish for you to stay on this path to liberation you now have chosen. Not freedom as a daytime reality show might advise, that would have you fleeing from a toxic marriage etc, but freedom from the past patterns that kept the world from getting the "fullness" of Leah. You can now shine and let us see your luminescence.

Frankly, the only perceptions I have of you from our limited interactions after a couple of shows, are of a rather shy, timid woman. It is only through seeing your Facebook messages that I know the kind of majesty, intelligence and warm soul that is there. No longer do you have to follow the story and lines others have written for you. Now, you can be guided by intuition and inspiration.

Leah De Luca   1/20, 5:31am

Holy shit, I can learn a lot from you. When I sent my first note to you to let you know what was happening with Matt and me, I never expected to find this amazing friend in you. Funny how you say you perceived me as shy and timid. Others in the "Matt & Leah" circle have said the same. However, in the "Leah" circle (my family, long-time friends, and in the workplace) everyone has always known the real me... someone very different than who I was when I was with Matt.

With Matt, I felt drowned out, diminished, sometimes embarrassed and on edge, yet I pretended to show the "M&L world" that I was happy. I use the "Matt& Leah" phrase because one friend of ours, upon learning that we were going to divorce said, "To me, you have never been Matt and Leah, you have been MattandLeah...one word." She said this with the very best of intentions, articulating her shock at our breakup and saying she always thought we were happy. I guess that is what marriage is supposed to be; two people becoming one but for me, it meant I lost who I was as a human being, because I know how different I am from Matt. Not better – different. Though I know I have many flaws too, I felt that MattandLeah was someone I did not want to be. Talk about feeling like being in a cage.

I can't tell you how much I relate to your story about taking crumbs and making them into cake. I too latched on to whatever good moments and behavior I could get from Matt. It was enough to get me through the next few days, or if lucky, the next few weeks of mediocrity and until the next inevitable "incident." Ugh...starting to despise what I am writing and I have to get to work but I'll touch base later. I can't wait to check out *The Moses Code*. Thank you for all these insights, I really feel like I should be sending you a check! Back later.

Craig Shoemaker   1/21, 11:15am

Please don't despise what you are writing! I love what you say. That you allow me to take part in your journey gives me strength. It reminds me how close I am to falling back into old habits that send me spiraling. If you open up, I do too. When I unlock the demons hidden deep in their hideaway, I command the life I richly deserve. Part of my insanity is having irrational expectations. To know this, is huge for me. How many times do I hold out for people who I think will see their errors and hence self-correct? I've had a lifetime of thinking the best about people. I still do but now have more realistic thoughts about outcome or the amount of time something will take to unfold.

I comprehend the old saying, "patience is a virtue" more than ever. But I still want the violators to learn their lessons faster! What makes sense however is to allow a wide space for people to find their own way. My impatience and subsequent panic exacerbates the problem. There is Goodness time and then there is Craig's time. I'm betting on the "Big G" to handle it. I heard once that the word "Spiritus" is a Latin word, meaning "breath." The practice of breathing more deeply, mindfully and consciously has certainly helped me through much anguish and many baffling moments.

Some of my defects that have incited a hellfire are; lying (whether directly or by omission), deceiving and being loud & intense. I can intimidate and don't even know I'm doing it. I give my opinions and leave little space for another idea on the subject. I squash when I should engage, thinking I know what is best for all involved.

Now I try to practice the breath of good spirit as much as I can. If a seemingly impossible duel is at a standstill, I go deeper into my lungs, take an extra beat and exhale with contrary action to what I normally would have done. Instead of getting over or past the turmoil, I go to a source that slows me down and lets me know all will be okay. I am an anxiety-stricken little boy, who runs and runs, so no one can hit the moving target. "Doing," instead of "being" is usually the order of the day. I spent a lifetime wrapped in fear, wariness and angst, and empowered others to tell me what was "correct" and how I should be. I bought into the concept that the more I had or did (or even "who" I did) would bring me happiness. I literally took my act on the road, where I could snow count-less women with intimacy so false and fleeting.

Yet, somewhere in time, the Spiritus kicked in. A drive for ascendancy began to be replaced by a need to slow down and listen. Whatever I wanted from someone else, I began to do for myself. The break I took in the action allowed for a kind and loving force to take over. Now when I see pain, I bring compassion. The person who directs anger towards me, I begin to view as a temperamental child, just like me. Stopping to reflect on the TRUE nature of the battle propels me into mindful thought and cognizant action.

Like any program or re-programming, it takes lots of diligence to master. I fail at dealing with difficulties far more than I succeed. Then again, the falls I take are the times I learn the most. When I first rode a bike, I had to learn how to balance, ever discerning what poor actions might lead to another spill on the pavement. Eventually, I learned that balance requires constant adjustment and that trust, faith and letting go of "thinking" are all that is required to soar.

I am a huge *Wizard of Oz* fan. I have seen the movie dozens of times, and it is actually one of the shining moments of my childhood; our fractured family gathering around the TV set to view it once a year around Thanksgiving. However, I have come to realize that this movie is far more than comfort food for me. It has become the parallel journey of my life as I think the author, Frank Baum intended; a fable we can follow, which leads us to our personal "home." My dreams really did come true, albeit in a much simpler and more delicate way than I had envisioned. I just wish I didn't have to endure twisters, flying monkeys and wicked witches to get here! Oh, and of course the best breath of all is LAUGHTER. Ha ha ha, ho ho ho, and a coupla la de das – that's how we laugh the day away, in the Merry Old Land of "HAas!"

Leah De Luca   1/21, 11:25pm

As you talked about your natural tendency to want to take care of a situation immediately, today I reflect upon how it is I will learn to hit my own "pause button." Oddly, this is not normally a problem for me because my tendency is to over-analyze and to get stuck in "analysis-paralysis." In fact, Matt was the first to file the complaint for divorce, despite the fact that I was the one who reached the conclusion that divorce was needed. My delay in filing was because of my inner turmoil.

But back to the pause button. Today I avoided the button and moved quickly. My attorney sent me the draft response to the misrepresentations and attacks on me, recently lodged by Matt via his own attorney. The response was very well written, much of it my own content. My attorney e-mailed the final version to his secretary to pretty it up and to send it out, copying me on the same message with a subject line that read "Letter to Adversary." Wow! Letter to Adversary? If that doesn't tell the tale, I don't know what does. The lingo boggles my mind. My adversary...my opponent...my "enemy." It just struck me as odd for some reason.

At any rate, it certainly set the record straight and that's what I wanted, right? Any normal person would not sit back while someone misrepresents the facts about them, and all the while with their hands out/open. Yet, why do I feel so bad?

Probably because in setting the record straight, more of the ugly truth is revealed. I know that the truth is hurtful to Matt and I honestly don't want to hurt him. Where is my breath of good spirit? Why did I not put out what I want to see in return? And here come those unrealistic expectations you talked about. I keep thinking that if I respond to these allegations, Matt will learn his lesson and he will stop this nonsense. He will "self-correct," man-up, and resume paying a fair share, or any part, of the family expenses. It might be frustrating for you to see someone like me repeating some of the mistakes you made, despite having the benefit of knowing some of your experiences and the outcomes. Like a child who does not hear or heed the advice of his parents who have been there before, I too, must test and navigate the waters. So be patient, as you may have to sit back and watch me fall on my face every now and then.

As we learn to ride a bike, we fall…but will re-adjust, develop trust, faith, and finally let go. I'm glad that you will not judge Matt, or me, when reading my story, and certainly, if you were talking with Matt right now, the story might be quite different. We are all on our own journeys; we all perceive things differently and through our own lenses. As with the bike analogy, I think I am still at the falling and re-adjusting phase. I hope soon to gain balance and develop trust and faith, so I can let go.

CHAPTER TWO

ILLUSION OF DARKNESS

Leah De Luca   1/22, 6:17am

And so I continue to search for peace. Each day something happens, small or big, that generates a myriad of emotions and feelings. Anger, sadness, loss, frustration, resentment, but at the same time, relief, a sense of promise, also remembering and missing some of the good things about the life I am leaving behind.

Last night my son's car broke down on the highway. The first call he made was to me. But really, I couldn't help him. Of course, I could call a tow company, and so could he. Diagnosing and fixing cars was always Matt's thing. Why didn't my son call his father? When I asked him to, I sensed his discomfort. Instead, he abandoned the car and decided he would call his dad this morning. I hope Matt comes through. In my mind he has bailed on so many other things since this all started. Sadly, each and every time he does this, I am certain he believes it is to punish me. I feel like he is saying, "Ha! Screw you! Now you'll see what life will be like without me!" As if having someone to plow the driveway, cut the grass and fix cars is worth trading for years of betrayal, lies and emotional abuse. I'm not going to lie; he gets to me. And now that I re-read what I just wrote, I think, *Come on Leah! You had more in Matt than a handy-man!* So there is that resentment sneaking out again, damn it.

Anyway, sometimes I rise above and tackle whatever comes my way with goodness and grace and other times, I allow my emotions to take over. Every day presents some kind of test for Matt, or for me. I know I'm much happier when my reactions or responses tip the scale on the side of goodness. Today, I am making a commitment that I will be true to myself. Hope you have a great day and inspire all you encounter.

Craig Shoemaker   1/22, 10:01am

I dig how you re-read what you wrote and it nudged you to look beyond. I think this dialogue we have will do just that – allow us to see past blind spots, and thus re-adjust upon further review…It just strikes me as sad though, seeing what you go through. I relate to what this does to a soul; so powerful and powerless at the same time. I ache for you, and for Matt, as I see two people, who at one time pledged lifelong love for one another, now positioning for war. I anticipate the ugly about to be unleashed, with both parties wanting their side told as they see it, responding to multiple years of horrible, stored-up feelings. Yes, it is inevitable at this point to defend using whatever is available in the arsenal.

Unfortunately, many will feel the effects of the collateral damage and very few are spared. The wrath of revenge is mighty. Hostility deepens the wounds. I know the trenches of divorce combat, and still deal with missiles launched into our home. Nothing can prepare one for an onslaught of self-aggrandizement gone awry. This happens in everyday life but add in unrequited love and the mix can be deadly.

Odd, in our justice system, we deal with absolute strangers speaking on our behalf, whether it's a lawyer, judge or "expert." Our voices, which have already been tossed aside, ignored and dismissed in our marriage, are once again shut down by courtroom proceedings and protocol. In 7 years in the judicial system, I've never been allowed to say a word. Much like in my marital relationship, it feels like none of "Craig" is heard. How many times do I want to yell, "That's a lie, that's not ME being described!" And just like my childhood, I'm put into a convenient compartment and told to be quiet. I am given the "rage" label, so all my feelings are disregarded. I have to trust a judicial process and a room full of egos.

One thing that rang true to me in what you wrote above was the part about your ex doing things to intentionally punish you. I swear, sometimes my ex is on a mission to dismantle me and sell my parts at auction. Then, upon further review, I can see how it has nothing to do with her doing something to me but all to do with her being the person she chooses to be. It's an internal ecosystem she won't address. Debby is similar to the climate change deniers, and will discredit anyone who tries to bring in logic. I still try to get her to look at how her selfish behavior is throwing our ecosystem off-kilter and destroying our family. Just like those crusty old asses in government, she reacts by coming after me, ignoring all pleas to be reasonable or discuss it.

But she isn't waking up every day and saying; "How can I get to Craig today?" My ego makes the assessment that someone is out to get me, when the fact is they are doing what they do naturally to sustain their existence. It's all they know in the present time. Most likely, forever. My ex sure does bug the shit out of me; yet I cannot afford to pay that emotional mortgage payment anymore. Letting go is the key and being self-actualized enough to comprehend the true reality, not the one based on false evidence. Now, regarding your kids…

My own dad left when I was days old and only came to visit on rare occasions, yet I have experienced recent epiphanies and revelations concerning him that I could never have envisioned. Sadly, today my father is riddled with cancer. I could justify my actions if I was distant or dismissive with him, recounting his absence and lack of care to rationalize my lack of love. Yet, I make my father-son relationship into what I want. Today I receive the kernels of love I had previously not seen, and it's enough and gratifying. Several months ago, I was talking to him about his cancer battle and offering suggestions to better his quality of life. One thing I asked him to do was turn off the network news, which apparently he was addicted to watching. I said, "No wonder you can't sleep, the last thing you are hearing before bed is death, destruction and mayhem. It's tough to put a restful head on the pillow when the last thing you heard was about a beheading."

For perhaps the first time in our relationship, he listened. He heeded my advice and turned off the TV. He slept better and more comfortably without the turmoil and loud blabbering of the news blaring in his head. It may sound simple but this connection with him was an amazing moment in my life. I'm glad I got to have this little nugget before he moves on from this world.

In addition, I had more great experiences with him once I opened up the lines of communication. I got what I wanted by giving. To be specific, one day he started a monologue about my wife Mika, waxing on about the letter she sent him that ended in "love you." He went on and on about the enclosed photos and positivity DVDs, as well as the caring note she sent that wished him well. He kept repeating to me: "She said 'love.' I haven't heard that in many years." About 10 times, he repeated, "Boy, that Mika, she's somethin'." I silently kept to myself that it was actually me who had asked her to send all that and that Mika had been following my wishes, since I was working/performing out of town. After many minutes of hearing how much my wife had moved him, I felt compelled to do something I had never done before – express my own love.

I said, "You know Dad, I love you." I kept saying it over and over until he semi- acknowledged that he had heard it. It was so powerful to drop all the old stories of his abandonment and co-create a fresh relationship. I spent well over 40 years thinking he should be more loving and that I deserved better but then finally arrived at a place where I don't have to be trapped in that system. Saying I loved him without expecting a thing in return, gave the power over to higher consciousness; one that knows the truth of the father-son relationship; two men, bonded in life through non-possessive love.

The rewards of our current communication have been astounding. Now, he and I talk as never before, and even more important, he has great conversations with my sons. This reminds me of what can happen when we get out of our own way. I say this to assist you in your own concerns about Matt and your kids (especially your sons), and perhaps to initiate a new way to look at it. Maybe my stories can assuage some of your pain over the relationship between your ex and kids.

I might add that men are different in how they deal with their emotions. We can take a circuitous and seemingly odd road to find our way home but the results are amazing. I implore you to stay out of the way as much as possible, allowing the men to connect in their own time and in their own way.

Leah De Luca   1/26, 5:57am

For now, I want to just thank you, from my heart, for your continued messages. I feel that I am by far the greater beneficiary of these exchanges and you have absolutely no idea extent of influence your messages have on me. You truly help me look at things differently and I desperately needed the perspective. Your views may be more objective than what I hear from those in my inner circle, because you don't really know me or Matt, and that's extremely helpful for me right now.

Craig Shoemaker   1/26, 9:58am

Do you realize that marriage vows ceremony was written long ago, and the life expectancy of a man was about THIRTY-SIX? If the marriage was starting to go in the tank, the dude croaked anyway. Maybe they should change the vows to, "Do you promise to love, honor and cherish, 'til…you don't feel so good?" I think Debby may have taken that "death till you part" stuff the wrong way. And if we are going with old customs, how'd that "dowry" thing not stick? Her only gift to me seems to be a hope for my early death!

I'm happy to hear you are connecting with what I write to you. Hopefully, through the bits and pieces of my life, you can find radiance where there might be the illusion of shadow. As far as men go, here's what I have come to know. Countless men have chosen the typical course of "scoring" wherever they can but they are actually left with emptiness and heartache. One reason this system of machismo does not work is that there is no end to it. Some spend a lifetime running from event to event, woman to woman, and are left unfulfilled and emotionally confused. After all, men are taught to drink, drug, fight, yell, bully, dominate and win-at-all-costs but at the end of the day, we still feel spiritually bankrupt. Men act like carpenters, banging, screwing and nailing – but without a strong foundation of solid materials of integrity, the builder is left homeless.

The first time I saw Kobe Bryant win a championship with the Lakers, the cameras rushed to him for his response to winning. Seconds after the final buzzer, he said, "This is great! And to all you fans, we're gonna do it again next year!" I thought, *Really? You worked your ass off to get to this ultimate athletic Holy Grail, and you took in the moment for less than 30 seconds?! At the top of the world and you are talking about the FUTURE??* Sound bites such as this help me chip away at some of the buildup of false beliefs about what would make me the happiest. I have my own anecdotal moments in time that led me to the removal of old ideas that were holding me back.

One example happened during the late 90s. My career was at an all-time high. Just like getting high, the buzz was fleeting and meaningless. I won two awards at that time; The American Comedy Award and the Best Picture award at The

Los Angeles Indy Film Festival. I made a vanity movie about my life and there they were, handing me a trophy for it! At the awards ceremony, I was backstage at the LA Convention Center, which was filled with 15,000 cheering people. Robin Williams was standing next to me, as he was about to receive a Lifetime Achievement Award. I wondered internally who would appreciate this the most. – *Who is the best person to hear this exciting news? My mom! My mother is the perfect one to let in on my bit of glory.* She loves Hollywood and movies, and I knew she would get a kick out of talking to a movie star too. So, I asked Robin if he would speak to my mom back in Philly and he kindly agreed.

With him standing next to me, I excitedly reached her on the phone saying, "Hey Mom, guess what? My film just won the L.A. Independent Film Festival and I'm standing here with Robin Williams, who wants to talk to you!" There was silence on her end, except for the sound of a TV in the background. "Mom, Robin Williams is here to talk to you and my film just won, can you believe it??!"After a long pause, she replied, "That's very nice, Craig. You know not to call me during *Jeopardy*. And it's the second round! I gotta go!" As she abruptly hung up I heard her yell out, "Who is Anwar Sadat!?" (She always, even in the privacy of her home, responds in proper question form.) In stunned silence, I stood there holding the phone as Robin looked at me. "My mom hung up, Robin. She's in the middle of Double Jeopardy." He gave me an acknowledging look of compassion and gently said, "I understand." Another moment of clarity – my mother will not become the person I want her to be, which means I (in turn) am doing what I despise having done to me – handing out a script and expecting it to be performed as I direct. Pretty humbling, ain't it? *I am that, I am.*

Leah De Luca   1/26, 7:28pm

Yesterday was a little rough, one of those days when I put myself out there with Matt, only to hit a brick wall. I dropped my daughter off at the airport. She's headed to Florida for an internship this semester. She had been nervous leading up to the day she left but within minutes of arriving at the terminal, she began interacting with several hot guys from Penn State, who were also heading there, leaned over to me and whispered, "Mom, I'm already likin' the environment I'm seeing!" It was funny; it was great seeing her be so excited and happy but it was also tough letting her go.

When I got back to my car, I was kind of emotional and the first person I wanted to share the experience with was Matt. I wanted to let him know what had happened and laugh with him about the new instantaneous friendships our daughter made. Impulsively, and ignoring the recent volley of letters from our respective attorneys, I typed a text message to him that in a nutshell read, "Just dropped Angie off at the airport, she seems so happy. In spite of all the pain we are both dealing with, the first person I wanted to talk with after dropping her off was you." I clicked the send button. Boom! It was gone. I waited. After a few moments. Nothing. Still today – nothing. The pain I feel when my communications to Matt go unanswered is pretty deep. I always wonder what Matt thinks at the very second he receives a message from me, no matter the topic or content. Here was a tiny chance for us to connect on something we have in common, the happiness of our child. I feel again that deep sadness I spoke of before. I feel empty. And so I dust myself off, yet again, and try to get back up.

As for the guy perspective, again, greatly appreciated and needed. I need to get better about getting "out of the way," as you so aptly put it. When it comes to our kids, I truly don't want to put Matt in a bad light and as much as I want to say I haven't done anything like that, I think it's fair to say that in fact, my behavior, my reactions, sometimes have. I'm not sure I gave Matt the chance to realize his full potential as a dad, perhaps because I took control of most things "parental." I would even complain about "having" to take that role and that too much fell on my shoulders but truthfully, maybe I enjoyed calling most of the shots in that area and wonder if Matt could have connected better with the kids if I had taken a different approach. My past does not make my future and I imagine that the kids and Matt will now finally have the chance to make their own connection without interference or influence from me. Could that possibly be a good thing that could come from divorce? I desperately want to identify more of the "good" that could come from all this. You give me hope. I don't want my kids to ever look back and think that I got in the way of that unique father-son or father-daughter relationship. Or that I eroded what they had or what they hoped the relationship could be with their dad. I think it's wonderful that you have found a level of peace and acceptance with your own relationship with your dad, particularly when he is grappling with cancer. But I must admit that in some ways it bothers me, only because it feels like you had to take those proverbial crumbs and turn them into cake again! I guess my hope for my kids is that they get more than crumbs but if they don't for some reason, then I hope they find a peace in whatever that relationship is or becomes. It all keeps coming back to wanting them to be happy. I also hope that they come to a place of understanding their greater life's purpose much earlier than I did.

I think you are right on the mark with all you reveal about the differences in men and how most are molded by our society. I accept the notion that the problems I have had with Matt may have little to do with me, and a great deal more to do with his own inner struggle. I continue to be amazed by your journey and hearing about the heights you reached in your career. The fact that all the successes were essentially meaningless to you without the greater fulfillment you were seeking, is something to learn from.

I was literally picturing you standing next to Robin Williams and what it must have felt like when your mom rejected what you were doing for her at that moment – basically, reject-ing you. While I'm sure it is difficult to let go of that family of origin, clearly, your newfound family is the one intended for you. The one who embraced and inspired you to be true to yourself. Your ex, your mom, your sister, your dad, they all helped you unleash what is real. And this "real" Craig is someone who now inspires me and countless others in a way that clearly wouldn't be possible otherwise.

 Craig Shoemaker　　　　　　　　　　　　　　1/30, 1:44am

I've come to realize that my family of origin is the greatest endowment of all. I am obviously saddened and often dis-heartened but the family who offered so little support caused me to find my own way. Hell, I had no other choice! I wonder if my mom and dad had dished out some loving behavior, would I have been driven to find this new place of freedom and bliss? If they had given me what I desired, I wouldn't have been forced to find a spiritual oasis, as my cup would be already spilling over with all my needs met and thirst quenched. This dynamic is the primary reason why I never hold back with a comedy performance. Ever. No matter how many people are in attendance or how much I am being paid, I give all I have on the stage. Maybe this is the reason I write so much to you. I yearn for someone to LISTEN to me. Ha!

I strived for "normal" for a lifetime, but had no clue what normal was. I learned to live in a world where the definition of normal was based on what I was a part of. Abuse became normal. Being berated – normal. Having my feelings dismissed and disregarded was the order of the day…every day. I now have a taste of what a new normal can be and it does not involve Craig being unseen and discounted.

When you wrote about "not thinking about a relationship," I identified with that. When I first separated, I thought I had seen my last marriage and that I was destined to carry out the rest of my days as a failure at having a partner. I blamed myself. Others blamed me too. I still hear, when dealing in conflict with my ex, "What did you DO?" I thought I was a loser and that no good woman would want me. I even harbored notions of getting back with my ex-wife, if she and I could just make a few changes. However, I went back to trusting that the Big G had my best interest at hand. I'd spent a lifetime of doing it my way, now it was time to ask him to take over. I kept repeating: "I know there is a partner out there who sees me for who I TRULY am." I have a mind-blowing story for you but have to sleep now. Goodnight.

Leah De Luca   1/30, 7:08am

Good thing I'm not working today – we had a pretty heavy snowstorm here! Like you, I really look forward to these exchanges. How is it possible that you have something amazingly profound to offer me, each and every time you write? You say your family of origin has been your best gift; the gift that brought you to this place. That resonates with me. While my own family of origin is very close and loving, I know without a doubt that much of my own life has been lived in trying to meet their expectations. At 55, I still sometimes feel like a 12-year-old around my dad. I continually seek and desire his approval.

For you, your family of origin was one of your greatest gifts in teaching you through some painful experiences – for me, maybe it was primarily Matt. But I feel a little stupid that it took me so many years to learn. I have something to learn about bravery. I did not have the courage to put an end to the madness for a very long time and for all kinds of reasons (maybe excuses, not sure). What was I in fear of? Being alone? Feeling like a failure? Letting Matt down? Disappointing others? I really don't know. I'm pushing to stop living in the past, learning from it but not living in it or being paralyzed by it. I still have some work there. I look forward to the days and years ahead, as I practice, "Letting go and letting God." Oh, and as far as the teaser in ending your message by saying you have a "mind-blowing story to share," as a result of turning your will over to a higher power…all I can say is, REALLY? You're going to leave me hanging like that?

 Craig Shoemaker   1/31, 10:57pm

Actually, I have been avoiding the next installment because it's very painful and emotional. But here it goes…

A few years ago, I was immersed in full battle mode with my ex-wife. Not only was there back and forth mud-slinging between us but her family members were brought in to attack from flanks I had not protected. I had a compelling desire to "tell my story" to those who had been bombarded by my ex's warped tales about me. I wanted my side told and as a bonus, I thought I could get her family to assist in speaking to my ex to get her to see the error of her distorted thinking. I wrote emails calling for an end to the insanity, telling the recipients to pull her aside and basically stop her from creating any more destruction in our family. I chose about twenty people to solicit. I was clear to make the content mostly about the welfare of the children, who were indeed suffering the consequences of parents on a drug-like binge of self-righteousness and justified anger. In the correspondence, I also threw in some anecdotal accountability, but the gist of all my communication was that my ex-wife needed to be halted and treated.

I identified her as the patient, even though I cleverly admitted some responsibility. One true conviction I did have was an offer to amend, change and compromise to put an end to the madness. I did what I could to sacrifice but needed the others to agree that my ex-wife needed big time help for mental illness. How do you think THAT went over?!

No one ever came to me and admitted that she was in need of hospitalization. Not one person laid any blame on her. What happened was that my intentions and subsequent actions backfired and exacerbated the problems. The email recipients refused to believe anything I said and used my words to give credibility to her claims that I was exactly the creep Debby said I was.

Each and every time I tried to get them to believe me, I was seen as a horrible man covering my tracks, who should be dealt with severely. They regarded my letters as evidence that I was a desperate ex, who needed to drive the scent away from his "real crimes." Subsequently, they painted me as a liar, a man of no moral fiber, and one who assigns liability to his ex-wife for his woes. Add to that, that I am successful and in the public eye, and even more folks come after you. I get compared to Woody Allen, Alec Baldwin or even O.J. Simpson! They believe a person of power to be able to influence others to stand by lies.

Worse, they used my history of being kidnapped and molested at thirteen years old to incriminate me as a pedophile. They *actually* used my worst days spent on this planet, a demoralizing, horrific weekend in Washington DC with a predator, and submitted it in court documents to try and demonstrate my profile as one of a child molester.

By the way, the case was brought to a mental health expert in pedophilia and my innocence was shown. It turns out my background is the OPPOSITE of the profile of a predator. However, this information did not stop my ex-wife and her team from using every conceivable ploy and tactic to incriminate me. They insinuated that there would be violence against me. I eventually used the recordings of their death threats to have restraining orders issued against my ex and two of her brothers.

Another defining moment of this painful saga happened in the office of our parenting counselor. My ex worked this woman with all she had. Mostly, because the doctor was not court-appointed, Debby used her usual ploy of threatening to walk out at the slightest provocation. One day, I blew up. I yelled at her, "You look me in the eye and tell me I molested those boys! Go ahead, you coward! Say I did those things to my face! Say it!" You know what she did, Leah? She actually lied straight to my face. And then, she went into her familiar rage mode and screamed, "Yes, you did! That's why my son has night terrors!" By the way, people of this kind of ego only say "my" when referring to children, forgetting there is a daddy.

Leah, it was as if she reveled in the thought of our children being molested or sick. I honestly believe that she projects her own issues onto our kids, hoping deep down that SHE will receive help for her mental sickness. Plus, she tries look like the hero, "protecting" her sons or standing beside them through their issues. One of the worst days of my life was when my ex-wife had one of our little sons put into a 72-hour lockdown in a mental institution for an "illness" Debby conceived and put onto our child. This was when I totally lost it. What she did was beyond comprehension. Her ugly deceit, lies and insane conflagrations had to stop!

Now, I need to have my own kind of stoppage. Fingers and eyes and heavy heart need a rest. I will return soon.

 Leah De Luca   2/1, 5:08am

It has to be hard as hell to be wondering what else she does to others when you are not around. I can see why you literally have to consciously work through what's happened, what's happening and what's to come. I am astounded at what you had to endure. To have what happened to you as a child used against you, in order to paint you as a person you clearly are not, has to be one of the most difficult things in the world. Did you ever think that the woman you once married could reach such depths of hatred? Against you... even against your children?

Your story makes me feel like what I am going through is trivial by comparison, though, I am now experiencing very similar circumstances in coming to learn that Matt is painting me as some kind of monster to his family; fabricating stories or completely misrepresenting what is really going on, and gaining momentum in rallying to his "team" anyone who will listen. (Ok, not the extent of what you dealt with, but twisted versions of the truth nonetheless.)

I stupidly thought that thirty years of demonstrated kindness, love, loyalty, responsibility, and accountability was enough to never shake anyone's perception of me. Wrong. And why is it that I care so much about this? I know the truth and that is all that matters, right? All I want to do is not care about

CRAIG SHOEMAKER

what Matt is saying, and who does or doesn't believe him. Very hard.

One thing I see from you is that you have really come to an honest and open place about your own role, your own behavior, throughout the process and journey. And you evolve from that. I really need to reflect and explore this more myself. Not saying that I don't already know some of my own flaws but I want to examine how my behavior may or may not be influencing Matt's. Am I inspiring fear, inciting anger or hatred in him? I know I don't want that. Someone I know once said, "If you want to keep getting what you're getting, keep doing what you're doing." If I don't like the result; the behavior that I see, it is I who must change something.

 Craig Shoemaker   2/1, 11:03am

Had breakfast cereal this morning. One thing I miss about being a kid is the excitement I had, knowing there was a prize in the box. Why not for adults? I'd love to get to the bottom and say, "Look…a stapler!" We have our own prize waiting for us, Leah, as we dig down and uncover. Knowing that you connect with much of what I write allows me to delve deeper and with more conviction, as I realize you are there to let me know this is a communication of higher purpose. I applaud you and thank you for the courage, to not only address certain aspects of my revelations, but that you honor me by speaking your own truth and acknowledging mine. From the bottom of my heart, I am grateful.

I envision a greatness in you that is begging to emerge. It peers out but has been put down by a myriad of forces. Now, gradually I foresee such monumental love and beauty for you; a brand new life, and one you could have never imagined. It's there. It's you. It might not be playing out in the ways you have become accustomed to. It may not be in a tangible or readable format at this moment. It will take much patience and a boatload of tolerance but your beacon is about to light up half of the Delaware Valley. I know it.

Had a thought today, as I started to think about my ex…Do you ever wonder if you hate them, or do we hate the fact that we married them? Do we dislike the behavior, or is it that we were fooled? Do I resent her or myself? Is it the fact that I compromised for many years and abandoned most sense of self, or do I simply detest her style? Do I judge her, even though I cannot stand being judged?

Wanted to say, before I write more, that today I am amazed at how far we've come. Only last March, police were at my home, taking our young sons out to our garage to interview them. By the way, the officer came out and immediately wrote a criminal report, not about me, but for "mother's cruelty towards minor children." Wow…even this guy, who thought he was here to deal with her not dropping the kids on time, got right away that there is nothing she won't say to innocent children to have them on her side and thus against me. I am even embarrassed to write some of the disgusting content of what she says I did, including, "Your father ejaculated on Johnny's shoulder!" Yup, that is cruel alright. Even to this day, when she feels cornered, she spits out these one-liners to cause a ripple and get people on her side. Recently, when an attorney was trying to negotiate child support modification, rather than actually finding (and KEEPING) a job, she changes the guy's course by spouting, "Craig has been anally raping our sons every day!" Every day?? I'm wondering how she makes sense of that one when half the time he's with her? Have I added magician to my skill set? I am apparently the David Copperfield of pedophiles.

When I write to you about these items, it does bring back some old feelings… yet, I think it important to never forget. Kinda like the Holocaust – it's a good thing to forgive but not cast key memories aside, for if not aware and properly prepared, similar atrocities can occur. A personal excavation; I think it's about unearthing, discovering and (then) throwing out our past garbage and emotional archives. The more we look closer at our conflicts, the easier we can get to the source. If I can stay cognizant as to my role in all situations, I can better manage any obstacle that comes my way in the future. Plus, it makes me move from dwelling on the ugly past, to appreciating the present. My knowledge regarding historical digressions allows me to better immerse myself in the moment, knowing that all bad feelings will pass. So, here is the rest of the story I've wanted to tell...

Throughout the years of separation and divorce proceedings, my ex-wife went on a savage mission. Somehow, she went from a general understanding that we were a couple with irreconcilable differences and a mutual agreement that our two children's welfare superseded all bad feelings, to an all-out assault on my character (and bank account)! As a result, I was obligated to pay for experts, lawyers, special masters, court costs, a full-time nanny, court reporters, mediators, retired judges and my ex-wife's personal attorney. It seems like a strange system, doesn't it? She comes up with any apocryphal tale about me she chooses and then I get a bill for the fiction. I'd prefer a Robert Ludlum suspense novel, thank you. She keeps coming up with sequels to *The Scorned Identity*.

In the divorce decree, I gave my ex a three-quarter of a million dollar home and paid her car and credit card bills, along with shelling out eleven thousand dollars a month for alimony and child support. My buddies like to say, "Shoe, I'll blow you once a month for that deal and I'll probably do it better and more than SHE ever did!" Of course, I agreed to this pact (not the buddy blow job) with the thought that this was final and we could all move forward but...seven years in and we're still spending our boys' futures on dealing with ongoing allegations coming from a person who shows few signs of stopping.

The worst part was the emotional waste and how much it hurts the children to be a part of all these ill-conceived actions. I was pissed, filled with rage and I hated her. I walked around with incessant inner dialogues, rehashing scenarios to make the hurt go away or to make her wrong. It was an internal struggle of reckless emotion. And that's exactly what she wanted; to know that I felt misery; to know that she was correct; that I was a mean man, who was not good for impressionable children to be around. I was indeed filled with resentment. However, resenting her was like taking a bath in a sewer and thinking she'll stink.

I continued to show up in court with hope that truth and my good intentions would be revealed, and that we could all move forward in a positive direction. Sadly, the family courts are akin to casino pit bosses, trying to keep you at the tables, knowing the longer you are prolonged, the more money they and their associates make. To top it all off, the legal system favors the mother. I checked numerous places and Googled the hell out of father's rights. Nada. There is only help for females out there. You won't find halfway houses for men who have been abused. Can you imagine a 12-Step meeting for male victims in Philly? "Hi, I'm Craig and I have been bullied by my ex-wife."...."Hi PUSSY!" There are literally tens of thousands of cases of women using/manipulating their children to hurt the ex-husband, concocting one tale after another but when the lies are found out, the women don't even receive a wrist slap. Maybe I should begin a movement that offers support for men going through the pain of being on the other side of women with Borderline Personality Disorder??

Even though I honored all my financial and other contractual commitments, Debby purposely did not take my name off the mortgage, nor did she pay nine months of house payments for the house I handed her. Coming from an impoverished background, where I actually thought the word "evict" meant "move," my fiscal achievements were a root and symbol of great pride for a boy who made good. Although filled with insecure feelings and fear of all being taken away, I built a life of security for my family. I saw to it that my sons will not have to be afraid of whether or not they'll find a safe home, or of having to go into their old penny collection to pay the pizza dude like I did. I set up college accounts for my sons so they'd never have to worry about making ends meet. My entire university time was spent working countless jobs, since I was the only one paying for the higher education. My mom and dad did not pay a dime towards my learning. This caused exhaustion and great stress, so it juices me to enable my sons to enjoy their university years to the fullest without the worry. When I was at Temple University, I even posed NUDE for tuition money, subtly pulling my pud so the artist rendering of my penis was "healthy." Tough to do in those cold rooms in the Philly winter!

This is my money background, so solid foundation in my adult years felt great. After my ex-wife's financial assault though, my name wouldn't allow for layaway at a pawnshop. But I certainly could not afford to stay on this path of destruction either. This called for bold and courageous actions. After all, there were young lives dependent upon my commitment to positive transformation. No longer did I yearn for sympathy or collusion, nor did I wish revenge on my ex. More than anything, for me, my family, my life…I wanted to laugh again.

Most people expect to have a laugh when they're around me. It's tremendous to know I can cause a smile or two, as I know that laughter enriches our souls. It's a great healer. For the most part, I have always found the comedy and humor in every situation, no matter how grave. However this time, humor eluded me. It's a stumper as to how to make light of false allegations of child molestation... *"So this pedophile walks into a bar..."* Still, not funny.

Leah De Luca   2/2, 7:48pm

On Sunday, I am heading to New York for a while, for a project at work. I swear the further you go in your career and the more successful you become, you realize that success is more about the ability to build relationships than it is your IQ. What did I just say? It's about building relationships? So much for that, given my present circumstances. Anyway, I just continue to be struck by all that you are telling me. It makes me wonder: What was it that she was truly after? Was she angry with you because you left? Was she jealous of what you have? What did she ultimately want from you and why? It blows my mind.

I am feeling this now with Matt. I was just informed today that although divorce proceedings are pending...he has ceased and desisted in any type of financial support of the family/household, and he expects me to provide "pendente lite" support to him right away. He does not care that despite my income, virtually all of it goes to take care of the family and all expenses. When my attorney reminded him of the costs for our sons' college/living expenses, his response was, "It was Leah who insisted our sons live away at college."...I guess he's basically saying if not for me trying to give our deserving sons the full experience of college, I could be throwing more money his way. Really? I have seen him behave selfishly during our marriage but this is more than I can take. It sickens me. He is an able-bodied man, capable of supporting himself, and it seems to me that he'd rather see our children give up opportunities so he can get more. I thought all parents wanted their kids to have more than they did?

You wrote about how the system favors women. I guess from my vantage point, I'm not seeing it. Instead I see laws that were probably set up to protect women who, for example, gave up pursuing a career to stay home and raise a family but it is these very laws that are working against me now. Only in my case, I don't have a husband who stayed home to raise the kids. Yet, he will use the law to his best advantage.

I think the thing that bothers me most is that I feel like Matt is clearly on a mission to punish me. It's almost as if nothing else matters to him right now. He must see to it that I suffer for making the decision to end the insanity. Do you think that is what motivated your ex? I can't tell you how much it irks me to constantly try analyzing Matt's behavior and motivation. I relate to your comment about walking around having these endless inner dialogues. I can be in the shower, or driving to my office or even in the middle of a conversation with family or friends, all the while having this "internal dialogue" you refer to. It can be torturous and you literally have to talk yourself off that ledge and make yourself stop. It's like the more you think about what's happening, or the incident du jour, or what's coming – they've won. They have the power over your mind. And when I say they've "won" I don't say it with the intent that we have "lost" because I'm not "in it to win it." That is clearly futile. I simply want the insanity to stop. I want peace and harmony, however, I keep fooling myself and wonder if this is actually possible.

I think the tougher thing for you, is that your kids are young and you have had to deal with your ex-wife on a much more frequent basis on decision making, and day-to-day issues involving your kids. I don't know which is worse...someone like her who is actively, but unfortunately, destructively parenting her children, or someone like Matt, who never cared to weigh in on anything of importance and often stood by criticizing. Still, when I think of all you have had to deal with when it comes to her...I am astonished at the person that you are right now. I know you have said that it is your ex who has been your greatest professor and that you in some ways were blessed to have had the experiences you had, in order to get to this place but sometimes I think, "ENOUGH!"

I also chuckle about the fact that people tell us to take or stay on the high road. I have people that fall into two groups: One says things like, "Turn the other cheek – take the high road. Maintain your grace and integrity." Then the other group (albeit smaller) says, "Fight! Don't lie down and die." Right or wrong, I am motivated by both groups. I have the tendency to want to be as fair as possible, giving more than I should, thinking that this behavior will bring about peace. When it doesn't, I need that minority group demanding that I take care of myself. This is what they mean when they say, "fight." They know I won't go after Matt. That is not me. They want me to fight for the kids and me. So, I am always balancing the need to make things right while not allowing myself to be trampled in the process. Easier said than done.

You have spoken often about not liking or wanting to be a victim. Interestingly, I feel less like a victim when it comes to all that Matt hurled at me during the marriage, than I do as I go through this divorce. What's that about? Maybe victim is really the wrong word. It's more like prey. I literally feel like Matt is a predator right now and I am his prey. Is feeling like prey the same as feeling like a victim? Because I don't want to be a victim either. I feel I am stronger than that and not accepting that title implies that I take responsibility for my own role as well.

I love how you basically say you are strengthened by your character. And I believe it wholeheartedly about you. I barely know you, yet, I am certain that you are a man of great character. I am going to start praying for your ex-wife. You too, but especially her. She may never come to realize the depth of hurt she caused/causes in this lifetime, but perhaps someday she will finally see things a little differently. It will be interesting to see what kind of relationship she maintains with your sons once they are young adults. Your influence as their father, and having them be witness to the love you have with Mika, is not only the greatest gift you've given them, but your greatest reward as well. More tomorrow.

Craig Shoemaker   2/2, 11:33pm

I think I am feeling the way you do when you read what I write. I'm really pissed at Matt's behavior! The part about him going after your money is bad enough but the stuff about him not supporting your kids though college is beyond belief. I'm really mad. It irks me to no end when guys abandon their kids. I am reacting the way I have so many times in dealing with my ex-wife. I want him punished. Damn, it's so easy to go there, isn't it? When I see injustice, I jump on it, try the case and hang the perp immediately. It's so hard not to take a side or form a strong opinion. I guess this also leads to an answer to your question about my ex-wife's motivation. It very well could be the same reasons Matt has for acting in such a deplorable manner. And yet, we will never come up with a good "reason" why they do despicable things.

I think my happy marriage now may increase the anger slightly for Debby but it's far deeper than that and it stems from way before I came along. I'd venture to say the same applies to Matt. We are supporting actors in their play and we perform many roles for them. Right now, we are the traitors who left them in a bind. We are the selfish creeps, unappreciative of all they have done for us, who will eventually find out how much we miss and need them. We have betrayed them and should and will be punished for it. As the author of the book, they must have the antagonist to show the contrast to the lead character, whom they make up to appear heroic and perfect to the outside world. We know the truth and that is a huge hazard to their system. I believe this is the primary reason my ex, my mom and sister will not go into a room with me. I am aware of their hoax. No one wants to be caught in a lie and one thing all who know me are clear on is: *I am a seeker of truth and will always ask the same of others.*

I have lots more to say but I have to hit the sack. Had a wonderful night watching our 7-year-old son play the Artful Dodger in the school talent show. By the way, this is the second week in a row watching a son perform in a school show, while sitting with my wife, baby and EX-wife. Much better. Yes, we have come a long way in ten months, since signing that custody deal. I even talked to her on the phone today too and customized some kids' plans without an unkind word. Amazing! Oh. Forgot to congratulate you on the career boost. It's actually a great thing to occupy our minds with something other than the intense tennis match that takes place between the ears. So happy for you that you pursued your passion and are now being rewarded for the commitment.

Craig Shoemaker   2/3, 6:01am

As the sun rises on the west coast, I have this thought: What if we looked at our former spouses as if they were the sun? That way we have a better understanding what their purpose is, and that their mission is not personal. If they are the sun, we do not question their actions. They merely do what they do. Their function is pure and gives us a life force. Without them, our families would not exist.

The sun has no agenda, even when it does harm to us. Inflicting pain is not its intention but injury occurs from our inability to respect and see it for what it is. It is filled with overwhelming, powerful heat and fire, so we must take precautions and safeguard ourselves. Like the ball of fire in the sky, we should never approach our exes without proper protection, and on some scorching days, it's gotta be a HAZMAT SUIT! If we do get burnt, it is our sole responsibility. Our experience is our ever-present warning. We must build our own home where our heart is, not on self-invested fears. The more our house is constructed on a solid foundation of integrity, sustainable materials and mindful design; the safer and securer we are. The sun cannot penetrate our dwelling, unless we are careless and don't do what it takes to insulate. We also possess the choice whether to open a window or turn on the air conditioner if it gets too hot. With knowledge, we adapt and find ways to deal with the sun's effects. If we lose sight of its power and think we can outsmart it, we suffer.

The sun and our former spouses can bring us light, nourishment and growth as no other force on this earth. Without this growth, we would remain stagnant. The sun stimulates a life force; to blossom and rejuvenate. No human capacity can combat the celestial power with equal force. In fact, you will lose all battles on their terms, so taking quality time to build our dwelling slowly and efficiently will lead to the most promise of keeping us from the effects of UV rays. In the case of my ex, it stands for "Uber Vicious," and the more I don't invite that heat in, the more comfy we all are.

If we are steeped in darkness, we know the dawn is inevitably coming. The hope of immersing in that glow inspires us. Despair is only a temporary illusion. The luminosity will always arrive each and every day. A cloudy day is temporary. The sun is still there. It's not hiding. Whatever is in the way can never own as much force as the sun, so we must always be informed of its impending reappearance. We can turn our heads toward the darkness, or look for the light. It is our choice. We may stare directly into the sun that blinds us, or we can use it to light our path. In the end, we cannot fully appreciate the sun's warmth, until we've frozen our asses off!

Oh Leah...you bring out the metaphor in me.

Leah De Luca　　　　　　　　　　　　2/3, 6:30pm

Are you kidding me? PLEASE tell me that you copied and pasted this sun metaphor from somewhere, because if you tell me you just came up with that quickly as you were writing me...

I love it. It is right on the mark and provides an easier way to interpret what I see and deal with when it comes to my history. When you say, "We re-wrote the script without their permission," you again hit the nail on the head. I performed in my supporting role just as he wanted me to for 30 years. How dare I ad-lib rather than follow the lines? His script would have him behaving exactly as he wanted to, whenever the impulse struck him, and then later admitting wrong-doing, asking for forgiveness, and repeating this cycle of dysfunction in perpetuity. I was re-reading your message about your ex-wife and her horrific accusations of child molestation. There couldn't be anything worse than being falsely accused of, not only of such a heinous act, but of committing it against the very people you love most in this world. I don't know how you can possibly sit at holiday dinner with her, or in the row of an auditorium watching your son perform, all the while knowing the horrific things she did. I may nominate you for sainthood.

Craig Shoemaker   2/4, 1:05am

Long day. It's hard to keep up with all the various ways of promo for my shows and I am overwhelmed by the amount of time spent engaging with fans. Exhausted and need a break. I'm starting my own social network called, "Quitter." Picked up my friend, Dave Cerami at the airport. I love him like a brother. He IS my brother. We met when we were boys. People like Dave really help me through this divorce. He offers only full and undying support, which is why he is family to me; Un-compromised love for one another. I cherish this friendship with all I have and I hope you can find this type of person to assist you through the confusing and difficult stages. It helps to know that someone is there for you no matter what.

As far as sainthood, I have to chuckle. Others might laugh at that too, witnessing my loss of calmness at times, while sometimes acting like a child not getting his own way. You should read some of the notes I send to my ex-wife. No lionized man would have sent them. I lashed out with vicious attack, thinking that I was justified to do so. One time, I was sent to a self-help weekend that was to help me get to a better place. After attending the seminar, I walked out mad that I still didn't get the solution I went in there for. One reason I acted like this was that I was afraid to open up wounds that

I'd ignored for so long. I felt that if I started to cry, I would be like a faucet with a broken shut-off valve. I have cried and mourned in the past, however, this one just felt like it was going to be the big tear dump that would not end. I was not prepared to go there. I started out willing and then slowly talked myself out of it. To top it all off, I had such a large boulder on my shoulder about victims…and grieving about self makes me feel like I am the ultimate victim. I resisted what I detest and didn't see how going there would lead to solution. The old habit of being a strong man is a hard one to break. I wrote a letter to my ex-wife and will describe it in more detail later. Bottom line, I recommend you write Matt a letter. Be completely honest as to your role in conflict. You don't have to send it. Just do it.

 Leah De Luca   2/4, 5:08am

Have to head out early this morning, but I am very interested in knowing more about the content of the letter and at what stage of the process it was sent. You are the second person who recommended that I write Matt a letter. I can honestly tell you that I generally do not lash out at Matt in any form, let alone at anyone else. Truthfully, I am not proud of some inter-actions I have had with Matt, especially before he completely ceased in communicating with me about a month ago. I know his vulnerabilities. Knowing his insecurities and how he has been riddled with guilt, I went and attacked him. When he shut down, not paying bills and began behaving selfishly and irresponsibly, I lashed out at him. My words were painful. I questioned his manhood, repeating, "What kind of man walks away from his responsibilities? What kind of man are you?" I kept saying, "Be a man!" I knew full-well how much this would hurt him, yet, I felt he deserved it. If you knew the extent of the passive-aggressive, emotional abuse I've felt during my marriage, this would seem inconsequential. But the differ-ence is, I put up with it for my whole marriage, so it became the norm. But for ME to react and behave this way, even just once, negates whatever overriding good there was.

When I talk with my family about my feelings of guilt for the things I said to him, they let me off the hook. Because they know what I've dealt with. They remind me that I am human and that I can only "take so much." Doesn't make me feel any better. So, I do want to apologize to Matt. I just want to be careful how I do it because right now, he is going after all that I have and I would not put it past him to use my feelings about him, against me. Any advice on this would be appreciated. I am fortunate that I do have close friends who are truly are like my sisters. They, my parents and my siblings are the ones who are supporting me, sometimes carrying me...and mostly, journeying with me, like you and your friend, Dave. I love them. I am blessed to have a circle of people who are filled with love.

Craig Shoemaker 2/4, 9:39am

One thing that has rung a bell in me is to simplify. Less is most definitely more. Clear out the clutter and allow the new to come in. Fortunately, Mika not only subscribes to this way of being, but also teaches me how to better do it. Who knew, after all the chasing, hoarding and conquests, that the tiniest moments would become my greatest treasures? Playing and laughing with good friends and family are the best moments and when in those moments, it doesn't matter a lick what kind of car is in the driveway.

Damn. I just looked at the mounds of essays to you, and it's NOT simple! I get on a run and can't stop. I realize there are key components/inquiries from you that I have ignored.

Now, about the letter I sent...

Basically, the content of the letter described the truth of what I have done to Debby and many others. When a person looks at me with harsh judgment, I am extremely uncomfortable. I become defensive. I know, strange that I would choose to be a standup comedian, a job that puts me in front of literally thousands of critics, but nonetheless I cannot stand being held under the interrogation light. I defend, using all available tactics to take the eyes off of me and prove their premise to be wrong. I fight back using a variety of methods but the crux of the matter is that I cannot take it when people look at me with presumption or assumption.

I do not like it when my covers are pulled, or someone exposes a flaw or misstep I have taken. I prefer I do my own unmasking, thank you, not have a self-selected evaluator dissect me. I don't like to be criticized, analyzed, scrutinized or chastised. I hate to be put under a microscope, and squirm to get off the glass slide. So, why would I want to do that to others? How would a man who hates having those things done to him, end up putting an innocent person on the pro-verbial hot seat, especially a person I love? Why do I want perfection out of them when I cannot come close to it myself?

If I don't like when my former spouse keeps score, using her list to get what she wants, then why would I proceed to submit my own card of stats that supports my desire for victory? Every time I think she is evaluating her card to beat me up, I am doing the same thing, even if it is silent. By the way, my silent thoughts of how fucked up she is, also tell the story of a man living a lie and the accountant in me will say, "But her violations are far worse than mine. She is by far the doer of unscrupulous acts, and her incompetence causes much more damage." If I do this, I am blaming. If I do this, I am being a victim of other people's insanity. If I do this, I am judging. If I do this, I'm asking for something they cannot give. If I do this, it causes others to defend. If I do this, I put a sharp eye on them, pulling focus from my own personal inventory. All of which, I admonish. *I am that, I am.*

One obnoxious character flaw I cannot stand in others is when they come from a moral high ground, and THAT was a huge thread in my 100-percent responsible letter to my ex. It's not the amount or severity or intensity of my arrogance that is important, but the fact that it exists and that someone on the other end of it is being hurt. I am human, just like she is, but here I was listing (either in my mind or outward) the things she did that needed improvement. As if anyone could make things better when I went about it in that way!

She thought I was a bullying, self-obsessed, know-it-all prick, and did not enjoy being on the other side of my righteous opinions. It matters not that her violations are more destruc-tive than mine. That's like saying my gun is a lesser caliber.

It cracks me up when our country behaves like this, calling citizens of Iraq "terrorists," when they are just using the weapons they have at their disposal. Just because they strap on a vest with an explosive device, does this mean our bombs that kill many innocent women and children are somehow more humane or just? It's still killing, and I kill my ex-wife's spirit every time I hold horrible thoughts or speak unkind words. I can hurt her by being quiet as much as she can cause harm by upping the amplification. Who starts it? Who cares? I've spent all these years portraying her as the instigator, when all I really needed to do was look within and accept responsibility. I re-created my childhood paradigm, using my ex-wife to play the part of my mom, hoping she could supply me with the comfort my mother refuses to supply. No wonder Debby is angry! I looked at her to love and support me in a way I had never experienced and when she fell short, it angered me. So, who's nuts? Me.

 Leah De Luca   2/9, 8:33pm

I've been getting adjusted to living in New York for a few weeks and REALLY liking it. Great distraction from all the chaos of the divorce. Enjoying spending time with some pretty awesome people. Although, I get my "back-to-reality" checks here and there. I just sent off a couple of e-mails to Matt about the need to communicate about basic issues like car insurance and the plumbing problems with our property. As usual, nothing. No response. It kills me. How can people shut down? No matter how angry he may be, I guess I just don't understand the concept. For me, it's just not an option. I can't figure it out and I need to stop trying to figure it out.

Still missing him, or the IDEA of him. Yet I realize each day that this was the right thing to do. Holding out hope we can be friends one day. I desperately want that. I want us to forgive one another and acknowledge that we had a life together that resulted in wonderful children. I want us to respect each other, care for one another as human beings, and build a future that keeps our family connected, regardless of our marital status. Maybe that's too much to hope for. Have I mentioned how much I loathe divorce? Just in case you forgot!

CHAPTER THREE

RESTORATION TO WHOLENESS

Craig Shoemaker   2/10, 10:38am

Just got back from an amazing trip to Kona with Dave. We got way deep, but mostly laughed our asses off. Flew back last night and hours later, I'm on a flight to Nashville. Was just in paradise, with luaus and charm, now headed to the Deep South, with storefront signs like, "Earl McTweed, Taxidermist & Veterinarian. Our slogan: Either way, you get your dog back!" Heavy road trip in store for me, which includes wintry Louisville, Lexington and Indy. Went from "chillaxing" in Hawaii to just plain CHILLY. I've turned into quite the weather wimp since moving to So-Cal 24 years ago. I'm going to write a note to you on the plane and paste it when I get settled. I remain enthusiastic and divinely moved to communicate with you and help one another get through.

Leah De Luca   2/12, 7:44am

Glad you had a great time with Dave. I don't know how many people you have in your life that you can fully open up to; people like Mika and Dave, but isn't it the best thing in the world? And as certain as I am about the deep and special bond you have with Mika, I'm thinking the longtime friend-ship you have with Dave has to be one of the most amazing relationships of your life. What are the odds of someone you knew as a child, turning out to be a lifetime soul mate in a sense? What draws us to our childhood friendships is so different from what we look for now in the people we choose to have in our lives. I'm always amazed when I hear that people have been close friends since childhood. That means the friendship has had the pleasure, and sometimes the pain, of being witness to most every part of our journey. There isn't much one can do or experience that the other doesn't understand, or call you on. And no matter what, our bond of friendship remains, always stronger and more complex than before. It's one of greatest blessings one can have. I think you have that with Mika as well, just not as long of a history. So you are doubly blessed!

I have a couple of people in my life that I feel this way about. People I am completely free to say anything to, knowing they will understand me, accept me, challenge me. Yet, I never had this with Matt. Our conversations were often superficial or dealing with just the "happenings" of the day. It was hard to really know Matt and hard for me to open up to him. I remember complaining to a close friend about this, years ago, and her advice was to look at the good in Matt and find other ways to fulfill what I couldn't get from him. She reminded me that no one, including me, is the "whole package." I bought into this somehow, yet, I knew I wasn't looking for the whole package.

I spent a lot of years yearning for a soul mate in Matt, something we were not capable of being to one another as a couple. I remember lying out loud – saying one thing, but feeling something else. You might think this is really strange, but it used to take me FOREVER to pick out cards for Matt, for his birthday, Father's Day, anniversary, Valentine's Day. I'm one of those people who reads all the cards in the store and has to find just the right one. What it says truly has to reflect how I feel about the person. I would stand there reading card after card, not being able to purchase the ones whose words read what I WANTED to feel, but truly didn't feel. Finally, I would find one that worked, that was honest, and still portrayed me as the loving wife I wanted to be. How crazy is that? I sometimes wonder if he struggled with this as well. So two things I'm continuing to work on; forgiveness and something you talked about, "to simplify." The latter is harder for me than the former. I want to simplify my life on a number of levels, not the least of which is focusing more on what I can give to the world rather than what I can accumulate. I have never been one for wasting money or being showy. Yet, in all honesty, I find myself falling into the trap of desiring more material things than I have. This is so absurd because I have never been gratified internally by anything material.

My greatest joy in life has ALWAYS, without fail, been based on the joy of relationships, feelings that I have done something worthwhile, or that I have helped someone.

So I'll be working on this, and I do think it'll help me come to grips with the part of my divorce that has me in the most fear, and that is that Matt will have me supporting him forever, taking as much as he can from me. On one hand, I don't want to roll over and not look out for myself and my kids, yet at the same time, I just don't want to care so much about this. Know what I mean? Anyway, more later. It's a beautiful day here in New York. I am going to head out to enjoy it.

CRAIG SHOEMAKER

Craig Shoemaker 2/12, 3:04pm

It always cracks me up to think how Dave and I initially bonded through immature and destructive behavior and now, we connect on such a meaningful and positive level. However, the laughs were and always will be the key component of our relationship. It's at the point now, where we can just THINK something and start howling. And what a hoot this latest trip was. Both ways on the 5-hour flight to Hawaii, zero headphones, all conversation.

I'm man enough to say this but we both cried on the plane, as we confirmed how much we mean to one another. I'm a sensitive sort and am tearing up even as I write this, as I recall some of what Dave and I discussed, and the obvious healing that took place at 30,000 feet. He mentioned that I have "always believed in him," and am the only one who ever did. It struck a chord in him and he did not hold back his emotions. Love was too powerful and could not be controlled. I told him how proud I am of him.

Men often appear to be shallow. I think it might be from covering up so much throughout a lifetime. There is simply too much dirt to dig up, so why bother? It hurts to take that shovel and unearth the parts of us that have been buried well beneath the surface. I was taught to accept the survival morsels that are convenient and easy to find but the wiser I got, I realized there was tremendous treasure to be found through exhausting excavation. Also, men do not choose to access the emotional trove that exists within us. We ignore what is right in front of us and hence look to alternative methods of going around the obstacles. I think this begins in childhood with the way we play. We might "want" to play house or doctor but our peers humiliate us and demand we participate in more "manly" events like contact sports. Games have an outcome. While in the midst of a game, there is little thinking about anything but what is directly in front of you. Feelings are limited, and are based on victory and defeat, and all other internal tenderness is beaten away and shunned by our fellow players.

We learn to conquer and spend much of our lives figuring out where we fit in and how we can best achieve superiority. Many never succeed, spending a lifetime running, jumping and barreling through with no purpose. It's a never-ending identity search. Unfortunately, we are not encouraged by parents or peers to look for other ways to fulfillment. We obtain approval when we receive some symbolic reward, which can be anything from a trophy, to a chick who plays the part of one. I'm guessing this is why guys cheat, as I have done in some past relationships. It is so ingrained in us to "score" with as many as possible, we lose sight of what is most important – our consciousness. We are hypnotized, comfortably numb, looking to outer fixes to make us well. Funny how we fracture to become whole.

Dave and I are becoming closer and closer as the years progress. Both are moving further away from our family of origin, and look to one another as a sibling who restores our sense of self. Dave also had a dad who didn't show up for a single event, remained "manlike" in keeping things close to the vest and never told Dave he loved him, even as his dad took his last breath on this earth. It pains my soul brother to this day, and he is not afraid to let me in on his psychological quandary. The disconnect between our organic selves, versus the person society tries to invent, is a key reason many are so angry and filled with rage. Our outlets are few, at least the typical ones that are in front of us.

I've been thinking a lot about Matt in this regard, about his obvious frustrations and lack of skill to move through. Yet, I've been extremely hesitant in speaking about him or lending opinion, as I find it hurtful when I perceive someone is taking sides against me, and wouldn't want to betray him in that way. That said; I am moved to help BOTH of you, as you both try your best to get past the tough times. My wish is for you to have peace and harmony, with a knowing that your love and imminent growth will help Matt, your family, and your friends and children as well. As your amazing soul emerges, so will astounding peace. All feel the tumult during this divorce, so why not now acclimate them to your newfound grace?

As always, I hope my insights can lead you to a greater understanding of what you are up against. Again, anything I say is not to demean him or collude with you. It's based on what I see from a heart's view. I just want you to realize that a man's journey is quite different than a woman's. What makes no sense to you might sound okay to me. I'll bet if you spoke with my ex-wife about her perspective, the feminine side would have a much clearer understanding as to why she has done what she has done. Perhaps, it's easier for you to walk in her shoes because you know what pumps and heels do to your feet.

It cracks me up when I hear about your difficulty picking out a card for Matt. I can relate! I bought eight gifts per holiday for Debby, in hopes that she would keep maybe two or three of them and praise me for my efforts. What that really says to me is how much falsity was at the core of our marriage. I had so many visions of who she was supposed to be. I went about my shopping based on fanciful ideas. Actually, I purchased several gifts that I had known my mother to like, figuring they had the same taste. And now I realize I was not seeing my ex-wife for who she was, but rather, as a fantasy creature that I could feel comfortable with.

So I'm throwing out the thought to you that maybe you might have a situation similar, and spent many years compromising yourself, adjusting and amending – all so you could make the marriage "work." I don't know, but I think it's worth exploring. Often, I find that a monumental discovery like this, with the impending healing that takes place after, leads to amazing good. Truth is an oasis of great nourishment, and is so appreciated after such a length of time rationing for survival.

Leah De Luca   2/14, 6:39pm

I met Matt in college and immediately after ending a long-term relationship. Matt was the complete opposite of my former boyfriend and this really attracted me to him. We were engaged three months after we met. He proposed to me at a party after having far too much to drink. Romantic, huh? It felt so random, in hindsight. I honestly knew nothing about Matt at that point. Stupidly, I said yes. Like in the movie *Jerry Maguire*, I think the marriage proposal was, "just a hypothetical." What kind of idiot was I? I almost hoped Matt would forget about it the next day and when he didn't, I think I went along with the engagement because I didn't want to hurt him. I was so intent on pleasing Matt that I didn't listen to my heart. But I'd be damned if I wasn't going to make it work at all costs! Some of my family members lovingly told me not to go through with it. I was pretty stubborn.

As I came to know Matt more over time, and during the engagement, I found things I didn't feel comfortable with but I felt I could change him. I realize now you can't change anyone – the focus has to be on oneself and not directed to others. One of my favorite quotes is, "Never underestimate your ability to change yourself, and never overestimate your ability to change someone else." I often wonder if Matt also felt he made a mistake in marrying me, and like me, just stuck with it as the honorable thing to do. I wonder if he stuck with it hoping he could change me, too? I don't know.

Thirty years of just "sticking with it" seems like a long time. Amidst all those years, we found an "existence" of sorts that became our normal. Not normal by any stretch, but our normal, nonetheless. There was definitely love in there too but I can't say it was the kind of transparent and genuine love that you clearly have found with Mika. I don't think I know what authentic and divine love is between a man and a woman because I'm still not sure I've ever had it. I would hope I would know what that looks or feels like but I really can't say for sure that I do.

Having and raising kids was the best part of my marriage. I was always able to keep the marriage going, no matter how unhappy I was at times, as long as the kids needed me. Of course, the older they got and the less they were around, the more I had to face the reality that I was with someone who I didn't respect enough and love the way I knew I should. Though I tried very hard to keep my feelings to myself, I'm convinced that my feelings revealed themselves to Matt in all kinds of ways. Whether it was a look I'd shoot his way while he was talking to someone, or my resentment that he couldn't take care of all my needs the way I wanted him to, or the fact that I often felt he paid more attention to other women, the bottom line is that I wasn't very happy. I pretended to be happy, though. I can see now that appearances were important for me.

I am holding on to your commentary that: "Maybe you might have a situation similar, and spent many years compromising yourself, adjusting and amending – all so you could make the marriage work." So while I can sit here and cast judgment on Matt for all that I perceive he "did" to me, it may serve me better to keep reflecting inwardly.

You are so right on when you talk about this bringing about compassion. I can't thank you enough, Craig, for helping me be more open to seeing what makes many men tick. I am not sure what state Matt is in right now. I just know he is really, really angry with me. I wish he had the benefit of your guidance and experience. Unfortunately, at this point, I don't think Matt has the skills and tools to put an end to his old self. It's all he knows. It's where he's comfortable. He doesn't see that if you want to get a different result, you have to change what you alone are doing. Still, coming to a place of acceptance for what possibly drove Matt to some of his behaviors, including my own role, does help me have greater compassion for him.

Leah De Luca   2/15, 6:43pm

While in NY, I had my mail stopped and arranged for a friend to pick it up every so often. Today she did just that and Matt happened to be there when she got there. They talked for a little while. When she called me to tell me about it, I was immediately filled with emotion. Having been cut off from any form of communication with him, I was anxious to hear how the conversation went. Not sure if this came from the fact that I miss him, or if it came from selfishly wanting to know what he revealed to her, or both.

At any rate, he confided to her that it wasn't right for me to put my grounds for divorce out there, given it makes no difference under state "no-fault" laws. Struggling with this one. In fact, I initially struggled on whether or not to go with "irreconcilable differences" (as he did) or to put my reasons out there, allowing myself to finally have a voice. I knew it would not matter in the financial settlement but perhaps I needed him to know why this was happening, at least in my mind. I wanted him to know how hurt I was. Truthfully, I wanted to stand up for myself. I wanted more accountability from him.

You've often talked about putting the truth out there with your ex-wife; trying to reason or make her see something she clearly should see, and how futile it was. Even how it often backfired on you. Clearly, this situation falls into that category. Now, I'm beating myself up for putting my reasons on the record because I know it hurt Matt. I expect the only thing I will see in return is retaliation. What else would I expect? Wish I had been further into our discussions before I made that decision a couple of months ago. That said, I have to move forward. Not sure when, but I know I have to ask Matt to forgive me if the way I handled the divorce was hurtful for him. I truly do not want to hurt him. I never have wanted that and this goes all the way back to that day at the bar when he asked me to marry him. Ironic isn't it? Didn't want to hurt him going into the marriage, and don't want to hurt him going out.

 Craig Shoemaker   2/15, 10:13pm

What you wrote fires off many neurons in me, as it is oh-so-familiar. Divorce is a new and scary place. There is no one to show you or teach you how to go about it. I have yet to see a class or an online seminar about how to navigate it. The only pointers we get are from those who will gain from it. The others who are weighing in will take sides and cannot hear the "opposition," blinded by allegiance. Incidentally, this applies to any breakup of a relationship, where there appears to be no good way to do it, without someone feeling the pain.

Most members of my support system were clueless, selfish or both. Some aligned with me. The lawyers fought to win, even as I stood by and held no desire for victory. There is an acronym I enjoy for the word "ego." If we are run by ego, it's "Edging G Out." The higher source is not in charge when we turn our will over to the orders of the courts and our attorneys or even to our own personal plan. Attorneys are not waking up each day, centering in peace and love. Contrarily, they begin and end their day by manipulating anything and everyone who is in the way. None think, *Hey, I am going to find faults in my client and show those weaknesses to the respondent.*

I would read mountains of documents and wonder, "Which one am I, the defendant or the respondent? Who started this anyway?" It's a veritable "chicken or the egg." However, in this case, the egg is smashed and the chicken plucked raw, no matter who goes first.

Ok, I am going to meander into the realm of advice giving…

First, I suggest that you not beat yourself up over any choices you have made. There's no reason to regret anything you have done. Choose to learn from it with ardent pursuit of truth and accountability. Remember, you do what you do based on fear of the unknown, and are doing so without the proper guides. Family and friends may have our best interest at heart, but are mostly clueless as to what is truly going on in your home and between your ears.

Next, if it is not too late, I would try to start fresh with a new and powerful foundation and intention, so that you can build a modern bridge. We cannot expect a single beam to be put in this passageway by our exes. If I could do the divorce all over again, I would have done what my instincts told me; what I did in the beginning, that is, seek (and stay with) mediation. Just the mere action of finding a mediator spoke volumes. I retained a mediator who specialized in divorce, whose partner was a lawyer who handled the legal aspects. Both were neutral, which is so needed when two people are so committed to making the other one feel more pain. If you can do a mediator, that alone will be a good step to melting the wicked witch that you might think holds Matt captive. The simple step of asking if he will get in there to hash things out will give him more trust, which has been compromised by you bringing up his demons to the court.

In the mediation, I recommend that you make a big-time attempt at humility and apology. Yes, even with him being a perpetrator of violence, you make the initial move toward the kind communication you seek. If he agrees to go in there, he will begin to grow. I suspect that right now he is doing what he knows how to do best, fighting back with vigorous vengeance. Beating you will now take a different form. It is all he knows to do to survive.

With my ex-wife, I have little patience. If I did, there would not have been such dire collateral damage. My EGO took over. Regretfully, I became stuck in the mantra… "How dare she continue to take me apart? I will not be a doormat any longer!" The thing is, if had I acted in the manner I desired for us to achieve, then I would not have been her punching bag (as much). Now, being guided by that which I wish to draw in, I am now (for the first time) behaving the OPPOSITE of how a victim acts. I am getting what I want – serenity. Within moments, I take us from being acrimonious to harmonious, if I get my ego out of the way.

Finally, BREATHE. Then breathe again. Ask the higher source to give you an understanding as to why Matt is utilizing these deplorable techniques. Then, forgive yourself for using tactics that have helped ignite Matt's misdirected feelings. Know that he is not prepared to "get it." Stick to the simple proceedings as shown to you by the experts. Start the healing by making this about YOU, not taking care of Matt's feelings. You standing for what is possible will initiate infinite potential. All will be the beneficiary of your steady resolve. Be the Leah you truly are. No more faking it by taking actions to take care of him. It will only incense him and hence, put you back in the miserable place where this originated. Please let me know your feedback on these suggestions. All questions are welcomed. List the obstacles, the confusion and the frustrations. Fill me in on some details such as if you can even utilize the option of a mediator. I want to hear as much as you can write. We'll get there....

Leah De Luca   2/16, 8:34pm

So my feelings are all over the place on this. My initial reaction is that Matt would not even consider mediation. Why do I think this? Because I believe he feels outmatched by me and therefore, I'm not sure he'd trust that the process, or I would treat him fairly. I don't say this to portray that I am highly intellectual or somehow superior, I am most certainly not. I just think that without trust, fear takes over and impedes the success of a process like this. My gut tells me that Matt feels he NEEDS someone in his court, on his team, fighting for and with him.

That said, I'm not completely opposed to putting it out there. I do feel like I'm so far in it with the attorney that I worry about this setting me back. One thing I am very anxious about is that this come to an end sooner, rather than later. My concern is that we would try this approach and invest in it, only to have it fail and have to start up with the lawyers again. Can you tell me why mediation did not work for you? Did that force the issue of having to go back to the more formal process? When I think of how shut-down Matt is right now, I can't imagine he would be open to trying a different approach. Part of me just wants to keep this moving and get it over with. I need to think on this more. Maybe I'm too tired to think clearly. Back later.

Craig Shoemaker   2/19, 12:49am

Actually, mediation was starting to work. I arranged it and agreed to go to mediators a mile down the road from her home, while I commuted sixty miles round-trip. I didn't want any excuses. What happened was that I began to date Mika and Debby found out. The shit hit the fan. Not only did it spell the real end of our marriage but it brought other elements to the room. Jealousy. Anger. Betrayal. These are the core issues for someone with Borderline Personality Disorder, which I believe she has. It is a feeling of a loss of control… and control they must. It is judge and jury combined. Folks suffering from BPD put all on a 24/7 witness stand, at the same time you're in an electric chair with their hand on the lever. These ongoing conditions were all accompanied by my ex-wife's hyper-managing me as to how I should introduce Mika to the kids and so forth.

She tried to manipulate how much time we needed till the boys met Mika, when my "whore" girlfriend could put clothes in my bedroom and when I could say she lived in my house. It was all brought up in the mediation with great tension, which delayed the process and caused more arguing. We spent several weeks just accepting the fact that we were divorcing, followed by months of her railing on me for anything and everything she could rile up in her drama-filled mind. We did exactly what we had done in all the rooms of couples analysis in the past, she brought the fire and I tried to put it out in any way I could find in my codependent repertoire.

It was all-symbolic of our previous seven years. She played the room with all she could muster up from her lifetime of being this distorted way. The tears flowed. The "justified" anger always poised like a bear trap ready to spring. Unfortunately, these experts didn't have a degree in lunacy. I don't mean just my ex. When I participate in the cycle, I drop intention for goodness and go to the dark side too. I let my fears run me instead of having faith and trust. I am hoping that you can stay steady within your convictions and take part in the process with knowledge that all will end up okay. The more I bite my lip, the better the outcome. Let her get in all the jabs and bullshit she wants. Whatever she says has nothing to do with the divorce settlement but I didn't have anyone telling me this at the time.

You have to know that you will not be left with zero. Actually, you will be granted a more whole self, and there is no price tag on that. Whatever you think you are losing, you are gaining a hundred times that, in building a new existence. If you approach this process as Matt's adversary, then universal law will come down hard on you. Energy follows thought and if you're thinking of defending yourself, then offending he will go. If you go in with the usual design of relating what you have been taught to execute, then the only result can be the same acrimony that led to the divorce.

With my ex, I fell off my foundation too many times. We both tried to have the mediators take our side, each of us, believing the experts were indeed aligning with the saner one. Ha! We were both acting like psychos! Oh, if I could do it over again....

Upon reflection, I certainly know now that a great letting go needs to take place. There is sacrifice. There is compromise. I didn't bite my tongue; I chopped it out. For this to work I knew I needed to drop many of my ideas of what I wanted and realize that there was plan of a higher power at play. It was imperative that I get out of my own way.

Freedom is the goal, not hurting Matt or getting something from him. You have all you need because you can now access the person you were meant to be all along. Love thyself and hence, an eventual partner will manifest. If I could do it over again, I would do much more swallowing of dignity, replaced by a heavy dose of humility.

To answer your other question regarding the ludicrous accusations...

One year after our separation, I listened to a voicemail from my hotel in Northern California. It was a message for me to call child services as soon as possible. I immediately phoned the social worker, thinking I was being asked to help someone. It was the worst day I have ever spent on this planet.

They told me that Johnny (almost 2) and Michael (almost 8) were at that moment being taken in for anal exams by Debby, due to a report they had been sodomized. I was thrown sideways. The Department of Children and Family Services woman told me she couldn't tell me anything because the report that had been filed said it was the father who was the prime suspect. She told me I was guilty until proven innocent. It was now up to me to show them I was not the culprit in molesting my two sons. She would divulge nothing more as long as I was under investigation.

I panicked, running a gamut of emotions while on the phone with this stranger. I was shaking and so upset, having no clue how to handle this one. The street-smart Craig, who had lived his life as a survivor, had nary a clue how to proceed. The only thing the woman told me was that it was not my ex-wife who filed the report, which added to my frenetic confusion. She said it was a "mandated reporter," Michael's therapist.

Damn, I was pissed! I kept trying to speak logically to the woman from DCFS but she wouldn't let me know anything. The more irritated and upset I got with her, the more I looked like the bad guy that was on her document. I tried to ask her to "be human" and consider the circumstances. To no avail. She hung up on me. From San Francisco, feeling so powerless and monumentally confused, I called Michael's therapist Harold Stuckey to get to the bottom of this. He didn't return a call for 24 hours, adding to the angst and internal torture. Leah, I thought I was going to die. Just writing this takes me back there, making me sweat and shake.

Finally, the "therapist" called back. He made it clear that as a mandated reporter he HAD to fill out this report, based on what my ex-wife had fed him. I asked him if Michael had ever said anything that raised suspicions. He said, "No." Then, I inquired about Johnny, who was not in his care, and he said he saw nothing wrong there either. He also stated that the anal exams came back and were negative, then told me that my ex-wife was UPSET at the results, meaning she was actually HOPING a child had been sodomized!

The more I spoke to him, the more I learned about what my ex-wife had done. She had been leaving our sons in the waiting room after Michael's therapy session, as she laid all this "evidence" on the child advocate. Weeks later, I read the emails she sent to this unqualified professional. Wow! She sent everything from a note I wrote to my assistant Little League coach about parents, to describing how she had tried to force Michael into some kind of "confession" about what she was thinking I did to him on our trip back east. She had lines in the email to this children's counselor like, "Michael, this is about what your father did to you on your trip, isn't it, Michael?" She leans on this innocent boy to mirror her words, then writes as if she's at the end of her rope with my abusing the kids: "Harold, I am now out of denial. I cannot let my boys go back there. Thank you for doing what you do. You are a hero."

Yes, she had her perfect patsy.

After getting the next move from my lawyer, I told Stuckey that we were going to court the next day and I was going for 100% custody, based on her jeopardizing the children's welfare by filing false allegations. I asked him to fax statements to me, especially the stuff about her anger over the negative anal exams but something smelled funny. He never did fax me. He also didn't call me back to follow through. I drove 400 miles all night after (somehow) performing in Marin County before an audience who gave me a standing ovation. I have no idea how I could focus on making people laugh when my soul was hitting a low I had never experienced.

That morning, Mika and I went to downtown LA to the court of Judge Stevens, a man I would come to know too well. I had never been to court before, so this was all so strangely new. I had no image of what to expect. My lawyer, Susan, told me to let her do her thing. She felt she had a clear case and that she knew the judge to be fair and child conscious.

I walked in and was stunned to see Michael's therapist sitting with my ex-wife! Seeing him there with her made him more like an emotional "TheRapist." I was sick to my stomach and felt my spirit dive even lower. Trembling, my mind was trying to make sense of what was transpiring. What the hell was he doing sitting with my ex? *Is she going down on that fat bastard to get what she wants??* I attempted to get their attention, daring them to gaze my way. Never a glance as we all waited for the judge to enter.

As I was about to find out all too many times, the honorable judge would not make a clear ruling. He delayed us to a future date, a move he rendered countless times throughout the years to follow. Also, a harbinger as to what was to come, he didn't let me say a word. I silently sat there and listened to the lawyers speak about us as if they lived in our homes.

I could not imagine how or why Michael's therapist would associate himself with my ex-wife and her false claims. What was he getting out of this? I phoned him and laid into him, forbidding him to see our child, wondering if HE was molesting Michael and that this was a cover up. Hell, I had no clue. I was frightened. The more enraged I got, the better my ex-wife looked.

I will get back to this story another time, but suffice to say a lot was revealed. Eventually, Michael's therapist confessed in a legal deposition that he had fallen victim to a great con

CRAIG SHOEMAKER

artist. A little redemption for me at a time where I needed ANYTHING to restore faith.

Leah De Luca   2/19, 1:15pm

Even though you explain what happened in great detail, it's so hard for me to wrap my head around what you went through. I know how much you despise the "victim" thing, and I certainly don't feel sorry for you or perceive you that way. It's more that I feel like I am coming to know someone of great courage and character. You beat yourself up a lot for losing your foundation and taking the bait when it comes to your ex-wife, but I don't know another human being on this earth that could have managed the ordeal you describe. Honestly. To be wrongly accused of harming the very people on this earth that you love most and to have a woman out there influential enough to have duped a professional therapist (mandated reporter or not)....it baffles my mind.

I guess ANYONE's life at ANY TIME...can be turned upside down if someone out there wants to hurt you badly enough. The fact that just recounting these facts to me brought about an actual physical reaction in you, tells me how difficult it is to put such a horror behind you. I again sit here in awe, wondering how you can stomach being in the same room with her, let alone holiday dinner I saw you having with her in your Facebook posts.

I do apologize if asking you the questions brought you to the painful memories. Yet something tells me it's part of who you are. As you have said many times before, all of what happened to you has led you to your life as it is today. Without it, you would not be here. Still – hard to be thankful for such horror. Why do some have to endure such pain before finding their true purpose? And while what I have on my plate pales in comparison to what you went through, I still see many similarities, especially when it comes to character.

Before I get back to the idea of mediation, a new letter arrived yesterday from Matt's lawyer. The upshot is that there are more lies and ridiculous assertions. The other side now agrees I should not be providing temporary support to Matt while the proceedings are ongoing but they continue to assert that Matt should pay for nothing. Nothing. Also, I am accused of making all decisions about our kids unilaterally and without consulting Matt. Anyone who knows Matt knows that if he does not like or want something, you WILL know it. I imagine this is to paint a picture of him being the victim, similar to Debby's earlier plight. He claims he has been "forced to find somewhere else to live" because I have threatened to "falsely accuse" him of domestic violence. This is insanity. For the first time in 30 years, and during these proceedings, I stopped allowing Matt to abuse me emotionally. I threatened to call the police if he did not stop confronting me with rage, following me around spewing foul and hateful words at the highest volume levels, and quite honestly scaring the crap out of me. To Matt, this translates into me wanting to "falsely accuse him of domestic violence." The letter goes on with lies that I cancelled his life insurance policy and other stupidity.

So again, I have to answer it. Money is being thrown away at will, because of Matt's refusal to communicate directly. In the meantime, my attorney wants to depose Matt sooner rather than later. Am I stupid to think that if under oath, Matt would actually tell the truth? It's the lies that send me reeling. I can pretty much deal with anything that is honest. I just keep asking myself, could Matt actually believe his own lies?

I used to say that Matt didn't bring me "up." I felt always a lesser version of me with Matt. But in retrospect, neither did I bring Matt up. Truly. My feelings towards him made him feel like a lesser version of himself, too. Owning up to my own role in the failures of our relationship is just as important to me as my desire for Matt to own up to his. I just keep going back to thinking how sad it all is. This, amidst the chaos of anger and waging the war you described.

So here I am back to that mediation thing...I just wrote, and then erased, three different beginnings to this paragraph. Why am I so torn on this? My urge to get this over with wants me to stay the course. I want to do away with the stupidity. I think I want to write Matt a letter. A letter that is humble, accountable, and reassuring that I am not here to hurt him. One that both gives and seeks forgiveness. My commitment to you (not that you need it) is that I am going to begin writing it. I am not sure how long it will be or where it will take me, or even if I will send it, but I'm going to write it.

Craig Shoemaker 2/19, 2:38pm

You're torn up because the world, as you know it, has been rocked. After having spent countless years doing it a particular way, now it's all turned upside down. How are you supposed to react to all this new and unexplored territory? Let me tell you, it ain't easy, and the reason I keep sharing is to assist you in navigating though this difficult time. The hope is that it will help you in finding yourself and limiting damage. I get it. Living with uninvited turmoil is a killer. I have so many voices in my head, come tax season, I'm claiming them as dependents!

To be clear, I am not beating myself up when I mention any time I slip from a strong footing in good spirit. I do it to remind myself where the real pleasure comes and how I need to stay close to what brings me to that loving place. Part of it is to get out the stuff that is painful. I actually get a lot out of it, so never think you are igniting something that hurts too much. Ignoring it only leads to a buildup of toxins. I cannot exist in a higher plane while operating in this old paradigm. How can I taste the now delicious food if bitterness engulfs my taste buds? The communication between you and me has become an outlet to salvation. Yet, there are still some residual feces from Debby actions that are stinking up my home. But my "hippie" wife took sage and burned it all over the house. That is a true story.

Always know that I hear you loud and clear and am happy to know you trust me. Please don't be afraid to fail or look bad with me. I hold no judgment. I'll never think less of you. Contrarily, I will applaud you for having the grit to try this an alternative way.

In fact, how about you write a letter that really gets all your resentment and anger out? Make it as juicy and full of rage as possible. It might help to start there. You can't begin a journey with forgiveness, which is something I found after much failure. Know also, that you don't have to send the letter. Just write it! There is literally a magnetic pull to contribute more to this dialogue. I have about 700 different email responses and Facebook messages to return, as well as endless work to do, but this is absurdly compelling.

I've been giving much thought to what you have written and I must say that your input, responses, thoughts, observations and emotional shares have been most inspiring. I have come to look at our communications as one of my greatest creations, since it comes from the "Creator" within me. This back and forth exploration of spirit has been so incredibly valuable to me. It keeps me in check. I am always so tempted to fight and win, but our Facebook confab takes me to new and refreshing dimensions. You know, after much thought and deeper knowing, I think that some form of this is the book I need to write. I'm starting to believe that this heart/soul/skull session is really a guide that can help others. I certainly have been published and have written for screen and blogs but have never expressed myself as I do here.

It feels enormously driven. Of course, not by me, but through a channel of the "Big G." Each time I write, it seems as if I am guided by that ethereal source, starting when I responded to your simple message telling me you were getting divorced. I still recall the acute drive that spoke to me at that moment. This is pure and profound – if someone reads it and it assists him or her through pain, then I have found true purpose in my life. If the reader indeed finds happiness or greater love, then my assist would be agenda-free. If readers have uplifting results, then I can be okay with the fact that I did not control or manipulate them into doing so. They read it, and the rest is out of my hands...

To me, this is about 2 humans falling, failing, flogging, flailing, flopping and fearing, who turn into graceful, grateful, godly, good, great, gifted, guffawing goof balls, who have a newfound appreciation and application for life. Through our discoveries, perhaps more can enjoy the fruits of the fertile land. We can support one another where we can't find it other places. I had so little, growing up; it will be a refreshing change. My dad used to tell me I was an "idiot" for having low self-esteem. What?? Obviously I prefer to move on from that logic and am drawn to your positivity. (BTW. Had no idea but according to spell check, "positivity" is not a word.)

 Leah De Luca   2/19, 6:15pm

I agree. I know what you mean about the magnetic pull. When I write, I am always thinking of the list of things I SHOULD be doing...even now, I'm leaving to go to a party and I have to cook some things, but then HAD to log on and see if there were any messages of inspiration from you. I also think how easy would it be to just pick up the phone and talk to you instead of writing but the writing has been so therapeutic for me.

When I talk, sometimes things just fly out and I don't pause enough to really think through what I want to say. When I write, my fingers fly across the keyboard – that's when I know I'm onto something very deep. At times, I go back and re-read, make small but important changes, and try to get my thoughts out there to you in a way that is more on point, more meaningful and thoughtful.

When I pause between paragraphs, there is a process that goes on in my head that is wonderful and one that I don't fully experience when simply talking out loud with someone. It is reflective. Craig, in my heart, I believe that as successful as you are with comedy, you have something AMAZINGLY more special to offer this world. I've just been the lucky beneficiary of your gifts in the past few months. I will be honest with you and have also thought about whether these exchanges could serve as something that could help others. But I have sometimes been tempted to delete the long history of our exchanges out of my fear that Matt could find a way to hack further into my personal life.

Yet, I am compelled to keep it. Because like you, it helps me. I re-read older entries sometimes because it makes me see the journey, instead of just today's latest challenge. The journey is much more compelling than any misstep or achievement of the day. I don't know what it is about your style that helped me open up to you, but again, it has been a gift of epic proportion. By the way, I like the idea of the letter that gets the anger and resentment out first. I think I need that. Then maybe an honest letter to myself (how weird is that?) and THEN, the "Dear Matt" letter. I'm all over it. I may work on this next weekend while on a brief respite with good friends. Thanks for the continued listening ear, support and friendship. I do trust you and so appreciate the fact that you don't judge. Also feeling pretty lucky to have found this outlet, your friendship, in such an unlikely way.

 Craig Shoemaker   2/19, 4:10pm

I wrote plenty of those letters. Pitifully, I SENT a lot of them. Some were deleted though, and those are the notes that led to the most positive movement. Once I press "delete," I have a huge grin. I know I'm doing something of more value than sending it to her. NEVER did any of my words, no matter how they were couched or cleverly expressed, elicit the kind of response from her that I had hoped. All that my letters do is arouse the beast. She sends them to friends and my family to show how horrible I am.

With any writing to self however, it is best to refrain from self-edit. Let this never-sent note be released from your core with a natural and unimpeded flow. Don't think. Do not delay. No grading of the paper. Just do it. You will find the first letter of expressed anger very effortless to write, as it's easy to access those feelings. When I say I fell from grace, the plunge was merely the upshot of where I was that day; forgetting to center in what is divine. With your current roots being founded in confusion, frustration, betrayal and anger, the product will reflect this. It's natural. Good luck. Now GO! Be ugly.

CHAPTER FOUR

STILL...CATHARTIC

Craig Shoemaker   2/21, 4:47am

Just had a thought. They call it, "dissolution of marriage." If "di" is a prefix meaning "two," then that would mean "solution for two." Right? Same for Di-"solve." You solve it together. We are coming up with a mutual solution for the problem – A formula that is the antidote to the poison we have been drinking for many years. Like chemists, we create a potion that dissolves the base of what has led to disaster, and now concoct a new design that gives us the answers to previous mysteries.

I think the key component is unconditional love. Most important is to love ourselves with abandon. We have spent too many years looking to please the owner of the lab, when actually we didn't see our own skills at making the perfect formula. We possess the ability to burn away all the elements that prevent purity. I guess you might say we distill it down to the basics. There's that "Di" root again. Add "still," and we have a recipe to live by.

Be still. My fear-based actions usually lead to more mess and compromise of self. Stillness taps into my source, which always has a greater good as the intention. Perhaps you and Matt can properly "digest" soul food without the nasty taste of all the unkind additions you both put into the mix that is your marriage. "Di" plus "Gest" equals...well...jest is humor... maybe you will begin to see the laughs in this equation? Swallow the concepts and man-made ideas and let in the goofy? Begin a diet of fun and don't take it all so seriously. Is that the key message we are to find? Ok. Maybe I'm stretching a bit...

Leah De Luca   2/21, 4:17pm

Flying into Chicago. Three of my friends are meeting me there. Just a short getaway with some great ladies, like the time you spent with your buddy Dave. We plan to spend the time reminiscing, sharing what's going on in our lives and saying what we mean to one another. But mostly, laughing and being silly. Per your advice, I plan to write with reckless abandon. I know that I won't send Matt the therapeutic version, the one where I let it all out. I need to do it and he certainly doesn't need to see it. But, I REALLY want to get the courage to write him a sincere letter and at some point. send it. I'll keep you posted. Focusing on myself and loving myself unconditionally aren't comfortable concepts for me. I am so much more comfortable helping others, working on their problems, lending a hand.

I spent a good deal of time in the past year of my marriage supporting a dear friend, someone VERY close to me who battled melanoma for several years. Then my cousin was diagnosed last year at this time. I poured myself into helping anyone who needed me. Driving my cousin here and there, sitting with her at medical appointments, helping my friend get through a rough time. All tough things, but doing whatever small thing I could do is what gave me the greatest pleasure during this past year.

Was I escaping from the final months of what had become a very bad marriage? I am good at helping others, yet so bad at helping myself. Several times in the past couple of years, Matt wanted to do a vacation or short getaway. There was always a reason I found that I couldn't do it. Not the right time, not enough money, I had this or that to do. Truth is, I didn't want to go away with him. I couldn't understand how we could go through constant marital battles that felt to me like pure lunacy at times…and then turn around in the next minute and want to be a 'normal' couple. I struggled with this. A lot. No idea where I was going with all that…sometimes it's just good to let it flow…as you say.

 Craig Shoemaker   3/3, 3:09pm

Tweeted this today: Superman, Batman & Spiderman all had no dad. Lesson? If you're a father; stick around. Or your boy will end up in tights.

Was just watching Tyler Perry thanking Oprah for encouraging people to write through their pain. Apparently, he heard her say this years ago and this inspired him to escape his hell by expressing himself on paper. Oprah used the word "cathartic" and he said he'd had to look up its meaning but once he did so he wrote like crazy, leading to amazing success, both inner and outer.

Hearing this prompted me to get back to my living catharsis in writing to you, which has taken a non-intentional hiatus. Yes, we get busy. We participate in the race. However, the more quiet and still I am, the better. The more I stay out of results, the better. The more I change my goal from one of "winning" to one of "serenity," the better for me and all around me. How many times have we seen fractured families ruined because a member chose to focus on some outside prize, instead of becoming a source of wisdom and truth by concentrating on what was right at their fingertips? While the ones closest to us pursue outside approval, here we are wondering why love will not suffice.

Yes, I watch Oprah. Not regularly, but I will channel surf and land on her show now and again. I think her popularity can be attributed to Oprah and her guests expressing themselves as the viewer wishes they could. She gives voice to hidden secrets that prevent most of our fellows from experiencing inner freedom. Today they were talking about men being molested as boys. As a man, expressing any kind of vulnerable feelings about the past is a tall task. It is so drilled into me to put on a good front that the resulting angry outbursts are not only accepted, but have become the norm. And so begins an insidious pattern; boy told by parents to cover truth, parents colluding with the lies, a buildup of resentment, a fear of never being protected, a relationship that is founded upon the lie of the unsaid, a codependence, a spouse gradually becoming part of the deceptive style of living, more resentment buildup, angry outbursts, excuses made for the rage, denial, protective defenses put up, fights about the ridiculous and obscure, a search for co-conspirators and then...all-out war. – All because of forming a union upon a pile of lies. A foundation constructed upon sand eventually erodes.

I learned too many hard lessons from not addressing certain parts of my childhood that I chose to ignore. I was so busy NOT being a victim, I forgot that I was one. I dodged my own feelings of betrayal and abuse and put them into "helping" others. It wasn't until 23 years ago, when I decided to stop doing drugs and drinking alcohol, that the real crap buried inside began to be revealed to me. All the time I'd spent pretending I was fine, turned out to be false bravado. I did what I was taught; put up a good front and walk with an air of confidence. Nothing bothered me. Yeah, RIGHT! Drinking wasn't the only escape, either. Putting down the bottle and the rolled-up dollar bill was a good starting point to clear away the mess, however, this was all a very grand plan from the "Big G" and the procedures were long and arduous. The pain felt each and every time I returned to what was "comfortable," grew with each act of abandonment of the self.

We owe it to ourselves to dig deeper into the personal land mines we place upon our paths. First I diffuse 'em by acknowledging they are there. The word "knowledge" lies within the word, acknowledge, so I assume it is great knowledge and good sense we attain by simply admitting something is present. No doubt, the consequences are severe if we choose to ignore the presence of an explosive device! I feel so much cleaner being honest. At our family dinner table with Mika and the boys, one custom is to state what we love about one another. Michael said, "Dad, what I love about you is how humble you are and honest. You always look to tell the truth, even if it makes you look bad." He made me smile. Of course, I don't just say things I think are truthful when it could hurt someone but self-inventory and expression of it does me a world of good. It's a wound that festers if I turn a blind eye to it. Deny its existence and beware of the scarring results. An abscessed laceration leaves a lifelong reminder.

My kids chuckle at me when I cry at sappy movies. One time, when Michael was around seven, he cued up the part of *Field of Dreams* when the Costner character, Ray Kinsella, discovers his father and says, "Hey Dad, want to have a catch?" My little bugger son knew that scene got me. So he says, "Hey Daddy, I have a Father's Day gift for you," then he presses play and devilishly turns to see me melt into mush. I bawled my eyes out and teasingly told him to turn it off. I've told Michael how much it hurt that I never had a single catch with my father and how my dad was never there for me. I constantly assure my sons that they must not let go of any desires or wishes they have for me to show up as a father, and to never withhold sadness or disappointment. Nuggets like that live in our hearts forever. Expressing my feelings reveals the TRUE me. That is who my children will get, as much as possible. No more fronts. No more acting performances whose scripts are written by members of society who know no better.

Ok. That's the end of today's catharsis. I've never seen a Tyler Perry movie or read one of his books but today, by witnessing his tenderness and subsequent evolution, his work has moved me to higher heights. Big G speaks through people, but can be better heard when the channel is clear.

Leah De Luca   3/4, 8:10pm

Funny, I also saw Tyler Perry on Oprah and was also very moved to hear him express the things that had happened to him. Strangely, I've been quoting you over the past few weeks. Things like, "simplify your life." You have no idea how your cathartic writings inspire me. Keep 'em coming.

Craig Shoemaker   3/4,11:55pm

It's been a week of teachings. I am attempting not to say "tough week," because I'm trying to see obstacles as mini-lessons. If something doesn't go the way I'd like it or want it to, I step back and look to an alternative way of reacting, instead of "traditional" responses.

Last week began by me hearing about a friend who died in his bedroom. I had helped Doug maneuver through mucho crap. He had it all at one time in his life; a house on the hill, great career in sports directing, money, Jaguar, hot women. Then, he came toppling down the hill and crashed, due to incessant drug use. Apparently, he didn't have "enough," and became addicted to cocaine, the fast lane to hell.

Like me, he had a difficult time with the good things. I identify with this feeling. It's strange, it is more comfortable when things don't go well because I'm so used to struggling. Adversity was something I could not only handle, but welcomed, priding myself on maneuvering through.

Doug and I worked through his addictions together, developing new skills and protocol. He cleaned up and began to rebuild. Yet Doug died just as he had turned it all around, making his death even more sad and tough to accept. The same day, my cousin posted about the twenty-year anniversary of his dad's death. My Uncle Alan was the biggest drunk I knew, growing up. He was also one of the only male influences during my childhood, teaching me how to shotgun chug a beer, as well as other party tricks a man should know. He was my idol and also (eventually) served as the paternal guide to show me what NOT to do, as the chaotic manifestations of his drinking caused so many problems for him and everyone around him. The funniest guy I knew, too. We all held a decades-long hope that he would get it together and become the man of his potential.

Like Doug, he finally hit bottom. Miraculously, he turned into more of the man we had prayed he would be. He stopped drinking, went back to college at 40 years of age, received his degree, fell in love, got married and worked a job helping other alcoholics recover. Amazing! He became a close friend, something missing in my family. Eventually, he helped me find my way through my first years of sobriety. I finally had a man in my life, from my family, whom I bonded with, and did so with more purpose and meaning. I now admired the real man he became, instead of inventing a man who existed in my fantasyland. Sadly, he died of liver disease, after six years clean & sober. The years of alcohol abuse had caught up to him. I flew to Philly to be there with him in the end, watching his entire system deteriorate. It was so harrowing to see him slip away – realizing anything I could do to save him was frustratingly beyond my reach. This was one the fixer could not fix. He passed and in the end, was so delirious he had no clue who was even there to love him.

To add to yesterday's emotional trifecta, my buddy since third grade, Rob, called to tell me he has stage-3 lung cancer. Holy shit! Not HIM! Such a healthy and strong man, always was. He doesn't smoke, making it more shocking. I've been through everything with this guy. We wrestled on the same team, him being a hero and me counting ceiling lights while getting pinned. We were housemates right after college; two guys about to launch into our careers. So many stories about Rob, and all of them pleasant. He grew up handsome & rich, but treated all with the same kind touch. His dad provided my first trip in an airplane, flying two 21-year-olds to San Francisco to tow big-rig, 16-wheeler Mack Trucks across America. Rob also helped build my dad's mule riding business with me on weekend trips to the Poconos, and remains close to my father to this day, often doing his best to have my dad drop the stubborn thing and get to know his only son. Ironic that my father chose MULES as a career, eh? Lol.

The one hope to hang onto in Rob's cancer case is that he and I talked at length about his approach to it all, and hearing him speak of his newfound direction and the invitation to let a higher source in, assuaged some of my fear. In all, the events of this week taught me how a new life is created – clear out the old dust to allow the beauty to be accessed. EMBRACE it!

CRAIG SHOEMAKER

Leah De Luca   3/6, 11:43am

Craig, I finally had the time to really read your last two entries in this living and shared "journal" of ours. Reading about looking at things this past week as mini-life lessons instead of as a "tough week," would prove to be valuable advice, as I had NO idea that this past week would stir up almost every feeling and emotion in my body. Sadness, anger, compassion, envy, joy – the whole gamut. First, I'm so sorry for the loss of your friend Doug. I'm guessing the hurt is compounded with the knowing he had just turned the corner. It's really hard to understand those who look only outward, and never inward. I am finding the more I reflect inward, the more I am capable of accepting and of forgiving.

I gotta tell you, I smile when you talk about watching Oprah and melting at certain movie scenes that make you think of something so personal in your own life. You often talk about the way you lived your life years ago, always out for winning the "game," for conquests, for proving manhood and strength. For me, I find myself drawn to men of STRENGTH. But strength of character, of conviction, of high moral ground… Strength of selflessness. A real "man" (and woman) to me is someone who knows the good and the bad and lives their lives ever acknowledging their shortcomings while in constant pursuit of something greater within.

One of the things about you that inspires me is that you are clearly on this endless path of inner growth and spirituality. You are extremely blessed to be raising your sons at this point in your life. Just think if you had been raising them while still in the storm of all past egocentric patterns and broken relationships? How lucky are your sons to have someone like you, with all the scars that made you what you are? I am so gratified to hear you say that your sons have the right to express their disappointment and their demands that you show up for them. Even more gratifying, is the fact that I KNOW you will listen to them.

I haven't yet put pen to paper on my letters. But I can tell you that I spent a lot of quiet time in Chicago last week, thinking about the things I want to write. I went back to the beginning in my mind, thinking about how Matt and I first met. I was struggling to remember EXACTLY when and where I met Matt. Anyway, simply going back in time in my mind and thinking about how things got started and how quickly I realized this was not the path I should be on, stirred up all kinds of emotions. I know I need to get them out.

I remember that so many things that went down between us honestly shocked me. Should've been a major red flag. One of the earliest arguments I remember centered around my lack of trust in him and the jealousy I felt when he had been out very late one night with friends. He came home pretty drunk and I should have known not to confront him in that state. Still, I pushed the envelope, as I often regrettably did. We fought...it was very late. Fighting with someone who was drunk, how stupid! At one point, I remember he walked up the steps and I was still at the bottom, yelling something to him. Instead of answering me, he stood at the top of the steps facing away from me, dropped his pants and mooned me. Sometimes, I actually laugh about it but you have to understand the world I came from before marrying him. I was raised by conservative parents who rarely fought (or if they did, we never saw it), they never cursed, and they very much isolated and protected us from anything "dark." I knew no drug users or alcoholics; I saw mainly pretty healthy relationships. Moreover, I was never exposed to "guy stuff," since I had only sisters, growing up.

Anyway, this early incident in my marriage was one of the first that demonstrated in my mind, the complete and utter lack of respect in the marriage. Maybe this sounds ridiculous to you – not sure. But I had never been mooned before in my life and for the first time to be from my husband, and in the context of an argument with him...I was not only shocked but that was the beginning of losing respect for myself and the beginning of hiding the Matt I was coming to know, from my family and friends. This was just the beginning...By the way, I've also never been mooned since! So realizing how silly this sounds, I am laughing my ass off! And that's a good thing! More later.

Craig Shoemaker   3/6, 1:55pm

Mooning...I must tell you, in telling me this story, you may have accidentally woken me up to a different perspective. I have to admit, my initial reaction was to laugh. I had a real, visceral and knee-jerk response. To be honest, my high school "Dungeon Gang" did a lot of drive-by moonings as idiot teens. I shouldn't do this but I tell those stories of pressing our ham on a car window to my kids, and tell them how we laughed at our black friend mooning too, asking if he was "eclipsing." One time I actually mooned a Philly cop!! We still share yuks about Officer McGinnis's reaction to being treated to a view of my teenaged alabaster ass! Then I read further into your story and had a different perspective.

At first, I thought Matt did something to diffuse and bring laughter to a situation, which is the way I handle many situations. Fights can become so ridiculous and off topic, often, I find myself taking them to a place that is more childlike. The core of it all is very basic anyway. Just taking it less seriously. Yet here you demonstrate that I should probably consider the other person's feelings before taking the juvenile route. Just because I deem someone to have ridiculous reactions does not mean that this absurdity holds the same thrust to someone else. You showed me how it could be interpreted as passive-aggressive. I get to look at it from another lens.

Maybe this is the magnetic force that propels us to write one another? Hearing such deep and explorative words from you, whose family of birth is such a departure from mine, shows me ways to revolutionary actions? Obviously, the reverse can also likely be true. I see my role in this as displaying a fresh reference for you, allowing you to inspect what it is that might hold you back from true fulfillment. In our special correspondence, we can offer one another assistance in an incomparable way.

You know why? Because nothing is heated. There is no "story" or history between us. Well, in your case, "herstory." There are no expectations, only acceptance.

I hold such a deep wish that my mom could see in me even the slightest bit of sparkle that you see in me. Here you are, someone I hardly know, seeing a version of me that is so much closer to who I actually am than my own mother deems me to be. I wrote her (yet) another letter to ask that we seek out a neutral party to sort through our differences. I just want to get in a room and put it out there but she refuses and remains locked in her righteous position. It is beyond frustrating and hugely hurtful to receive "zero" pride from my mom, let alone love. And to refuse for years my invite to discuss it safely, in a room of her choice, is simply heart breaking. Logic Boy sees no reason but a step back reveals a mom doing all she is accustomed to doing. Incidentally, there's another slant where I might raise your awareness, that is, concerning addicts. You said you were raised without witnessing it, so maybe I can help you notice Matt's way of functioning as a manifestation of something besides what you might think it is. Since you spent all those years somewhat insulated, this could be the education you're looking for!

Leah De Luca   3/6, 5:53pm

Ok, so I'm seriously glad you laughed out loud about the mooning! I knew you would! I have to add that now that I have raised sons, I clearly have had to develop a different perspective on not just mooning but also on farting and other bodily functions! Still, I do appreciate the fact that you get the difference in the scenario I described, and can see it from another vantage point.

You know, you really deserve the love from your mom that you desire. My gut wanted me first to say, "Try to move on and don't worry about it, because you have the love of a wonderful wife and children." But that would be shortsighted coming from someone whose parents saw and still see the best in her. The love we need and expect from our parents is just as important, regardless of our age, as the love we give and receive in other relationships. And I can see this is a difficult and ongoing struggle for you, and one you're not willing to (and shouldn't) give up on. To be honest, I'm sad for your mom. She has absolutely NO idea what she is missing in you.

My kids are nowhere near perfect. I've never been one of those moms who was blind to her children's faults, and we of course have moments of mutual frustration. They have failed me, and I have failed them. Still, I adore them. There is nothing that I am more thankful for than being a mom to them. Even when they disappoint me or I disappoint them, we come back to a place of love and respect for the people we are.

My wish for your mom is that she will begin to see who you really are; who you have become, and will be able to sit back with the kind of pride that fills my entire being when I look at my sons with all of their goodness, flaws and imperfections. I'm really glad you haven't given up on her. I don't know if there is something I can offer you from the "mother-son" perspective, but I'm here for you, as you have been for me.

I have to agree with you that these communications are extremely special. And not having expectations makes this easy and still so meaningful. You have no idea how your perspective has already helped me.

One other very important thing I forgot to address is your comment about addicts and the possibility that I take note that Matt's way of functioning may be a manifestation of something besides what I think it is. You hit it Craig! In the short time I spent working with a therapist, I had been describing all the behaviors about Matt and she very quickly categorized them as "addictive" behaviors, saving me the suspense of my agonizing over whether if I tried "just ONE more time... would I be hurt again?" And you know, maybe it's not just Matt! Maybe I was addicted to being and feeling in control by being the center of our family when it came to the kids, decisions, etc.? Matt often referred to me as the "hub" of our family. He meant it as a compliment; however, I recall it bothered me because I resented that I was a woman who carried most all the responsibility on my shoulders. Yet, deep down, I also loved this characterization. I think I was an enabler...big time.

 Craig Shoemaker   3/8, 2:15am

I'm literally writing you on a cathartic emergency basis! It's two in the morning and I am up in a mental tizzy of epic proportions. It frightens me to return to the old days with my ex-wife, complete with a hundred versions of speeches I want to give to her. I simply cannot quell the ramblings in my head, which is why I am writing to you.

I let Michael in on it too. He drove with me to an audition yesterday when I did a "big no-no" and told him about one of the recent fights between his mom and me. Of course my suspicions were correct though, as my ex already had him read the email that caused this week's battle. She has been letting Michael in on our personal battles since he was a baby but that does not justify the fact that I brought him into it. So, there is amending number one, when he wakes up – let him know how sorry I was that I involved him.

Amendment number two, affirm my commitment and progress in moving forward, grounded in positivity. Amendment number three, stop trying to do what a higher power should do. Step back and let go! Keep my yard clean. Don't tell people how their landscape would look if they took my advice. Amendment number four, let my ex-wife ramble and *do not respond*!

This week, things got really heated. As much as I think I didn't show anger in my notes or messages to my ex-wife, or as much as I believe I come from a good heart, the bottom line is I too lace words with venom. I get high & mighty; ironically, exactly what I accuse her of. Yes, I project my own shit on to her. *I am that, I am.*

We can start there. I tell her to get a mirror all the time, bugging her to start looking at herself, when it is my own deflection over to her that is inciting the mess. I speak of her being a dime-store therapist, when it is I who am the self-appointed counselor. I talk about her anger and here I am, very angry. I talk about her attacking, and here I go, leaving stinging messages dressed in a supposed wish for peace. I speak of her arrogance; yet speak to her as if I am one with all the answers. I become incensed when she brings up history and yet I ignite her rage by reminding her of deplorable actions of the past. I talk about her believing she's right and here I wax on about how right I am, showing her how much worse her offenses are. I go off on tangents that have nothing to do with the present, just as I say she is doing. I ask that she not involve others, yet I ask my wife, Mika to get involved. Debby uses dramatic words. I use words to raise the stakes. She gets people to collude. I get you to align with my thinking. I go nuts when she includes Michael or Johnny, and there I was yesterday, asking this boy to step in and talk sense into her. Ouch. That hurt me even writing this truth. I know better than to include a child in our battle.

Leah De Luca 3/8, 6:24am

So glad you expressed what you're dealing with. Oh, and I don't see it as you asking me to collude with your thinking, so go ahead and cross that one off the list. Like you, I'm not going to judge, or at least I will try. As I get to know you better, my urge is to want to protect you, side with you, but I know you want truth. The good news is I don't need to give you

CRAIG SHOEMAKER

much of the truth because you're so good at working through this stuff that you bring yourself exactly to the place you need to be. Amazing. Anyway, I do hope you are sleeping as I write this. I love the affirmations and amendments. I understand the feelings of guilt when it comes to the occasional setbacks with kids and in involving them. We're human. And you already know how to make this right. You're an amazing father and though I admit it is worrying that the occasional chaos still has influence on the boys, I also know they will be fine. Better than fine, because they have you and Mika!

"This above all: To thine own self be true, And it must follow, as the night the day, Thou canst not then be false to any man." ~ *Hamlet, Shakespeare*

I think the hardest part for you, and to a lesser extent, me, is navigating these waters with someone who hasn't the capacity for, or is unwilling to learn, to grow, change, or forgive. It's so frustrating, and yet all we can do is accept this reality. These limitations push you… me…us to continually take the high road. I don't know what's worse. Your situation, where you're constantly battling with your ex-wife, or my situation with Matt, where there is zero communication. I tested the waters yet again on Sunday night when I sent him a short email message letting him know a message had been left for him about a job interview. I ended the missive with a simple, "Hope you are well." And, yet again, nothing. Every time I reach out and try to open the door to communicating, I end up feeling like a fool. Matt remains in a very angry state and cannot separate the emotion from what is real. I often question myself about how I could have entered into a marriage with someone who feels "entitled."

As I've admitted before, I think I knew from early on that Matt and I weren't right for one another. Time and time again, we proved this to each other…Yet we kept it going. Going back to my message the other day, about reflecting on my own marriage – it started without trust and early on, I realized there was a mutual lack of respect. If I try to understand what motivated some of his behaviors and couple that with an understanding of some of his emotional challenges, it brings me some element of peace and it helps me on the road to finding forgiveness. I am not angry with Matt for anything that happened during the marriage. I am angry with what is happening with the divorce, but I'll get over that too.

Craig Shoemaker   3/8, 10:30pm

What caused the recent upheaval is that I initiated contact between Mika and my ex-wife. It was a mistake on many levels. They sometimes deal with one another regarding homework and such and in this case, I asked that my wife follow through on another Debby mistake. Debby is so disorganized and hadn't checked off boxes regarding something from Johnny's school, choosing again to ignore that the boy has a father too. Mika got reamed by Debby for being "challenged."

My sweet wife is apparently going deeper with her role in all this, and the revelations are excruciating. Deeply affected, Mika has wept over the hurt inflicted this past week, as Debby verbally abused her again. I went blind with anger. Not rage, but anger. I think this is why I was up late last night. During her mini-emotional cleanse, Mika brought up some things about being the perfect child for her mom. She is the first-born of seven, and was brought up in an unusual way in Japan, having an American mom and Japanese dad. She became the caretaker early on and I'm guessing this is the precipice of a great unearthing. I should not have allowed my ex-wife to just do her thing. Let the sleeping dog lie? Nope. I had to go there, which is an indication I must not be completely on the other side. We are in the midst of a throw-down now, and the only victor in this will be Debby. I'm sure of it. I put a wounded leg into shark-infested waters. It's now a feeding frenzy. And the moron I am, I wrote ANOTHER letter today! I should know better. I too must look at how much weight I chose to put on this crap. The heavier the weight, the harder the fall...

Maybe I need to feel the sorrow. I go so fast to the solution that I end up avoiding the true feelings of the little boy who was left alone to fend for himself. I've never mourned this part of my life. I've skimmed it but never surrendered to the intense feelings of a child forgotten and dismissed. Perhaps this is the missing piece to my wellness. It's easy for me to become mad but to cry about my plight is almost impossible. Instead, I go to this area of guilt, thinking about how there are so many with more weighty problems than my silly issues. Moreover, I feel obligated to show my kids strength and resolve. The last thing I want for them is to pity me.

The good thing I have observed is that our boys have been especially delightful and seem healthier lately. More smiles and more joy. The calm I desired and fought for in court for the children is finally being realized.

CHAPTER FIVE

WEALTH... AND POVERTY

Craig Shoemaker 3/9, 9:43am

Had some thoughts in the shower, where I do my best think-ing. It is not the ideal place to hang for long, having an eco-friendly wife, however, my new perspectives regarding the case with my ex-wife incite her to waive judgment. She is so funny sometimes with the New Age stuff. Mika says, "You know it's spiritual to fart?" I said, "Well, you just married the DALAI LAMA, honey! Get under the covers; I'll give you a Dutch Oven. You'll be praying, alright!" ;)

Anyway, today I was thinking about people with a great deal of wealth. You may not know this but currently, I'm trying to secure money for a feature documentary about the healing powers of laughter. I have an all-star team in place to make the film, an incredible script and inspiring agenda, however, I have been unable to nail down funding. I've been at it for years, met with various money people, but have come up empty.

So, what is the reason the same cats keep coming up with oodles of cash to fund projects that don't touch the integ-rity and promise of our piece? I boil it down to one thing... our focus becomes what we manifest. For example, when I put energy into eating, I become heavy. Likewise, if I put energy into what I don't have, indeed the result will be more lack. Sounds odd to think of "more" and "lack" in the same sentence but I have long held the belief that I will have a lifetime of financial struggle and indeed I will. Even with my trio of trial; my mom, sister and ex-wife, I have spent decades seeing what seemingly cannot be delivered – hence no deliv-ery is made.

I'm left being mad at the manufacturer when in truth, it was me who ordered the limited service. I ask for less and I get less. I am so busy putting energy into helping or assisting others, I forget to tend to my own basic needs and expe-rience emotional bankruptcy due to mindless withdrawal without restoring the funds. However, the rich dudes get up in the morning and plan their day around money. They arrange meetings about it. They check in on it. They take actions to acquire more of it. They train to adapt to any situation or obstacle that prevents them from having it all. With this knowing, I can better comprehend where I am going today.

Today, I look to grow my love, and tend to my garden with great nurturance. Seeing Mika and my children blossom over time makes me believe I have a helluva green thumb! I stay still to hear the great source within me. The divine tells me to be of service and approach others with this same kind of compassion and understanding.

Craig Shoemaker   3/10, 8:14pm

Leah, I am once more in need of a letting go! Remember when I wrote before about how I felt protective of Mika and pissed that my ex was putting her emotional bullseye on my wife? Well, Mika just phoned me. The worst happened. She was three months pregnant and just now miscarried. We lost the baby. My friend is driving me back home from Orange County right now. I am rushing back as fast as I can to be with her.

To be honest, the stage of grief I feel is anger. I want to call or write that witch Debby and tell her she's done more damage to us than she can imagine! It's been over 15 years of constant harassment from this woman. Why can't she move on? Why doesn't she get a damn job, or find another man to bother?! She is so sick, the way she keeps battling. My buddy Bob went through very similar turmoil in his custody battle with a mentally ill ex. He is very succinct in telling me not to go there. I'm writing to you to calm down at his request. I am so sad right now. Will talk to you later.

Leah De Luca   3/10, 11:58pm

Craig I am so, so very sorry. There aren't any words that could possibly lessen the loss you and Mika are experiencing. I understand wanting to direct the anger at Debby. But just don't do it. It's hard to imagine the emotional roller coaster you've been on these past couple of months. Listen to Bob. Listen to yourself. Listen to the "Big G."

I also implore you not to go there with your ex-wife on this subject, not now, not EVER. Write a letter and shred it, if you must. But you and Mika will heal and while stress can do all kinds of damage to a healthy body, the reality is you don't know if this was inevitable. Let go, and let God. Don't let your ex-wife enter the conversation between you and Mika when you are discussing this loss. Don't allow this intruder (i.e., the rage and resentment) to take root or to have any place at the table on this very personal time of healing in yours and Mika's life. Let go, and let God. I know I have only come to get to know you better over the last few months, Craig but I have to tell that in reading what you're experiencing, I find myself filled with emotion and with concern and love for you and your family. Is that even possible? No matter. Just know that I am thinking and praying for you all. Amidst the turmoil, the sadness, the loss, there remains so much beauty and love in the Shoemaker family. New life will be yours again and it begins with healing of mind and body. Peace. ♥

Craig Shoemaker   3/11, 8:22pm

Spent the day hanging with Mika. It is difficult for me to watch the woman I love go through such overpowering sorrow. It really kicks in the rescue guy and I honestly wish the pain could be transferred in some way. If I could, I would siphon her agony into my bloodstream. This is something that engages the powerlessness in me and my surrender is key.

Walking the earth with Mika is a gift. Somehow, even sharing this very difficult moment is okay. Because of this foundation, we get through anything together. I truly appreciate your kind and thoughtful words. I have calmed down from the pissed-off stage, dialed up the Big G and asked to have my tumult tumor removed. Indeed, my wish was granted, as there is a sense of profound serenity in our home tonight. Thank you for doing your part in making that so.

Leah De Luca   3/12, 4:06am

So glad you're back in that "place" where you belong. Are there any other men in the world that have evolved to where you are? Anyway, I'm still in Delaware, heading back to NY later today. Before the news of your loss, I had begun writing a new blurb that I put on hold but will resurrect it and finish it when I get back to NY. Also, I realize you are still going through the loss, and if I'm ever off bounds and not being aware of what you need, please let me know.

Craig Shoemaker   3/13, 2:02am

I have been up half the night with a mind monologue in my head, keeping me awake. Yes, I have the tools to return to a healthy rest but tonight I am subtly choosing to pull out the dull scissors to excise the damage, actually believing that this time it will work.

I am into it with my ex-wife again. She is coming at us, even though I clearly keep telling her to stop. She smells blood in the water and is circling. It's her natural instinct. She's the only one who watches *Jaws* and roots for the SHARK. I say I want none of this...but then...do I? I must evaluate what it is that attracts me to this conflict. It ruins my day and that of those all around me when I engage on her terms...and her terms take no prisoners. I know better. The last time I involved myself in this kind of dogfight I ended up losing all of my money. My reputation was sullied to detestable proportions. Even worse, the fallout was damaging to the children, perhaps even for a lifetime.

In our latest round, my ex-wife refuses to stay within the court's contract and refrain from calling our house. The loss of our baby and Mika's being distraught over Debby's mean-spirited assaults, caused me to draw a stronger line in the cement, asking that Debby and I communicate through emails or text messages, instead of leaving voice mails. I did this logically, knowing that a paper trail allows for fewer misunderstandings and less volatility. Sure, sounds easy...."Wish on one hand and crap on the other, and see which hand gets filled first."

Wishing is something I have done for a very long time. I wished for my dad to show up. I wished for my mom to care about me. Wished for more money, hot girls, even stability. Wishing is for losers. Fantasy. Yesterday, I had no coins for the wishing well, so Johnny did what I did as a boy and started fishing with his hand for change in a fountain. He wanted to make a wish, holding a belief that his dreams would be realized if he chucked a lucky penny into the recycled, bubbling water container at the car wash. I told him how I used to do the same thing at Plymouth Meeting Mall when I was a boy but didn't tell him how I used the money I pulled out of the water, which had been put there by other people. I'd see a guy toss a quarter in the water, and say quietly to myself, "Looks like MY wish came true! Another game of PacMan." I suppose my wish for money was instantly granted but got traded off for long-term bad karma, since it was stolen money.

CRAIG SHOEMAKER

Nowadays, I can't steal, borrow or glom on to a wish and hope it comes true. I have to "be" the desire and let the astonishing actions of a greater source unfold their beauty. If I choose to be grounded in the purpose of doing good, I know good things happen. If I can be present, magnificence presents itself. If I serve to others, I watch it pay off in spades with a constant happiness that's pervasive in all my relations. If I let go, all around me are less tense. With these reminders I am feeling much more free. Better, I am sleepy now, the insomnia is now gone. Small miracles...

Leah De Luca   3/15, 6:56pm

Mahatma Gandhi said, "Be the change you wish to see in the world." This sums up what you are suggesting to me, and I thank you for that.

Craig Shoemaker   3/15, 9:24pm

I am on social networks too much. You know it's bad when your son tries to get your attention by giving you an invite to the dinner table on a Facebook comment!

Had a scrumptious day. My friends from Philly came in (broadcasters for the 76ers), and I took them to an amazing golf course and made them "a big ole' Shoemaker meal" after a round. I love to cook, especially for great friends. I have always nurtured friendships; they are literally family to me, making this day off the charts. I am feeling really great right now. Can't say the same for Mika, though. Even my buddy Marc noticed it, pulling me aside to mention how she looks devastated. She is going through hell at this time. I ache for her.

Last night Mika took an hour or two to make the healing about me, giving me the ultimate prize – a massage. During our intimate late-night moments, she was so expressive and caring about how I too needed to grieve and "get it out." Instinctually, I know I need to have a good cry. I realize that expressing the difficult emotions will help me get through this. However, I just don't want to go there. What prevents me from having the internal freedom that I crave? Maybe I don't want to feel sorry for myself. I notice extreme guilt as I even write of my problems. I prefer to take care of others. After all, "I should be over this by now. I'm a grown man." One part says, "Go for the cry! Let it out," but the side that wins is the one who retreats from looking further into pain. Also, I fear that I won't stop bawling once the floodgate is opened. Like it might hurt too much, so I keep a lid on the penetrating emotions. Maybe this has something to do with my ongoing invite of ex-wife's shenanigans into my world, or maybe my mother stuff or both? Who knows? The answers will come when I get out of the way and allow them to come through, unencumbered by fear or judgment.

 Leah De Luca   3/16, 3:49pm

So sorry to hear about Mika's continuing struggle. Her spirituality and the gifts she's been blessed with will help her work through the healing process, yet it doesn't make it easier for you to witness her pain, I'm sure. What a giving and loving person she must be to turn the focus from herself to you, even amidst her own pain. She's obviously extremely special.

I find it interesting that you've been unable to cry in spite of all that's been hurled at you. You come across to me as someone who is very strong, yet somewhat fragile at the same time. And I say this in a good way...though I know you're not threatened, as some men would be, by that assessment.

Anyway, I will tell you that this weekend was a little rough for me too. I think I experienced true loneliness this weekend. I often felt "lonely" during my marriage, but in a very different way than I experienced this weekend. I was literally aching for Matt. Driving in my car, sitting in church, walking outside, out for dinner, I was missing him. I missed the smell of his cologne, I missed resting my head on his shoulder, I missed him squeezing my hand in church in a way that meant, "I love you" or "I'm sorry." I missed hugging him. I am crying as I write this. Still, I know I don't belong with Matt as his wife. What am I missing? Is it the familiarity? The comfort of knowing someone was always there...toxic as things often got? I often refer to the "good Matt" because there was, there is, a wonderfully good side to Matt. I just savored those good moments however frequently or infrequently they came along. I don't know. I'm sort of a rambling mess. I'll be back tomorrow, hopefully with a new outlook.

Craig Shoemaker 3/17, 10:39pm

Reading your last note I was beginning to well up. I became sad for you, knowing how the ache is being felt so deeply. I honor your process and am so pleased you are choosing to walk through, and not around, what is present. I truly identify with the missing and longing that comes up through divorce, especially when we are alone and undistracted by work or events. It is bound to happen.

I believe we gravitate to what is familiar, to what we know. We develop an adaptive lifestyle that includes on-the-spot forgiveness and an openness to change our actions to make the situation better. I frequently took on the role I was cast as; "bad guy," looking at how I had done something wrong, and then finding out where I could improve the equation. I sacrificed what I wanted for the goal of peace, often eschewing my personal thoughts and beliefs for the greater good. I worked under an assumption that my partner would eventually get that I was there to stay and did all in my power to improve my actions.

It was all based on the ever-flipping moods and whims of my (then) wife. I frequently held onto the notion that if I did so, all would be okay. I denied my own inner guide and conversely turned life over to someone whom I deemed to know more than I did. I didn't trust myself. Even went to others to support some of her opinions. I picked people who were similar in approach to my ex. What I forgot to do was consider the messenger. These were people who accepted paradigms of living that called for little growth, seeing life as less than that could be had.

The word "potential" contains the key ingredient of "potent." There is not much fire, thrill or potency in a life lived to please others. Their complacency becomes contagious, as we go unfulfilled and unsatisfied. Now I realize the magnitude of what can happen when we wash off this old slime. When we're not kept down by fear-based design, extraordinary things can take place. The scary part is to truly stay in faith and deep belief that we deserve and will receive what the good Nature wants for us. My truest self cannot express itself, if encumbered by fright. I used to question those who wrote books or espoused theories on relationships, and even poked fun at their credibility. Most of the time when I looked further into the person with all my "answers," I found someone whom I did not wish to be like. I began to value me, more than the me others desired. My family wanted me to work out my marriage. They wanted me to see the error of my ways and stick it out. Why repair what is not broken? Thankfully, I came to realize that I am whole, unique and filled with good spirit. I didn't need to depart from who I truly am for the sake of another person's damaged ego. Likewise, when I try to convince or change someone into something they are not, it spells danger. I did this with Debby and am still stung by the results of phony, self-obsessed actions.

I guess I am writing to you with some purpose, to let you know that the best is yet to come for both of us. One thing I've learned through all this is that the more we center in the omnipotent power, the more absolute beauty will appear. There's that word "potent" again…

CHAPTER SIX

LAUGHTER THROUGH TEARS

Craig Shoemaker   3/25, 10:07am

Last night, I was performing at one of my favorite places in the world, the Comedy/Magic Club in Hermosa Beach. Being on that stage is like being at home but I guess not the home I'm from, since these people actually listen to me, love me and let me speak freely! My first time there was as an audience member back in 1988. I went to see two of the hottest comics of that time, who were enjoying success as cast members of *Saturday Night Live.* One was their news anchor, the ultra hip and thesaurus-thumping, Dennis Miller. The closing act was a guy on fire, mostly from a character that caught on and became part of our cultural zeitgeist – "The Church Lady." The very talented Dana Carvey was the headliner, and brought the house down every time he broke into the catch phrase, "Isn't that special?" New to L.A., I was in awe of what I was seeing on stage and in the audience. The place was on fuego! I can still recall the unique bond between audience and performer, which began with a ten-minute opening act from someone no one had ever heard of…David Spade. He looked so young. His first line was, "Hey, I'm David Spade. I'm TEN. My mom dropped me off here. She's grocery shopping at Ralph's." I remember thinking, "This guy is like watching a quiet storm!" When I eventually got to know Spade, I nicknamed him "Q.S." for Quiet Storm.

Subtle and understated, but the laughs he received were ebullient. What a treat to observe their effortless connection with the audience. To be part of that, and having no pressure to perform, was really cool. I was an anonymous participant, yet my only requirement was to go with the gush. It is pure joy to be a secondary part of something like that.

To me, "LAUGH" is an acronym. The L in Laughter is "love," because the vibration makes you feel and touch all emotions within us without worry or doubt. It's pure and beautiful, just as love can be in its effortless moments. It is "Acceptance," since everything in that instant is exactly the way it is supposed to be. It is "Understanding," in as much as some great force, a natural connection, takes place between mind, heart and spirit. It all fires simultaneously, resulting in a reaction of a smile, a chuckle, a snort – visceral responses to something said or done that our deepest self comprehends. It is

"Gratitude," because every time we cry out with emotion, it acknowledges our appreciation for nature's gifts. Only humans can truly laugh, and we are fortunate to be able to express ourselves in this manner. It is certainly "Humility," and we are always reminded how our ego takes us from a higher source. Conversely, our falls are a constant reminder of just who (or what force) is really in charge.

Yes, comedy is a spiritual experience of an alternative variety. Most don't really get this, neglecting to see their humorous holiday as anything beyond a night of escape. We are so grilled from birth that the only celebration of a deity can be done in a church, mosque or temple, but I see a comedy club as providing similar lift. I'm reflectively memorializing that late 80s nugget. Nights like that are special and "wholly," the type where you remember who you were with, sharing that unrepeatable time through eternity. I hold clear visions of that evening, not only because I experienced great joy, but also because I committed to do what those three comics were doing. That is, providing the stimulus for hundreds at a time to be elevated, preferably on that stage in the South Bay; a place that has launched so many incredible careers.

It was a special moment in my life, an exciting time filled with promise and aspiration. It was also my second date with a beautiful, vivacious and glowing young lady, who looked across the table at me with unsaid words saying, "I like this and I like being here with you." Who, you say? It was my second date with Debby! Yup, there's the humble part again. I thought this would be the woman who would share laughs with me for a lifetime. The joke was on me!

Leah De Luca   3/25, 8:30pm

I have sometimes wondered about what it's like for you to be in your profession. One thing I never really pondered, but have come to realize in getting to know you better, is that you HAVE to be extremely intelligent to be a comedian. You talk about the effortless connection with the audience that you observed with David Spade back in the day. I so relate to what you describe about losing yourself, for that instant, in that inner "comprehension" of what you hear or see, triggering whatever the response.

I have to ask you. Do you ever feel that you always have to be "on" to the outside world? I think about how difficult that would be, and then I realize that being a manager, responsible for 80+ people, I myself feel that I have to be "on." I do let my human side show to my staff, but often feel the need to protect my staff by showing my "strength." Part of why I became so adept at hiding the problems with Matt. One by one, they express shock and disbelief when they learn of my impending divorce. They must have perceived me to be someone without problems – not sure.

As for me, I am carrying a lot of guilt and sorrow for some of the decisions I've made during this divorce process, especially for hitting Matt with the counterclaim full of detail of the things he had done which when combined together, constituted the grounds for what the law calls "Extreme Cruelty." I told you previously about my intention of writing him a letter...I started it, but haven't finished. Knowing Matt as I do, I don't think it will be read and will most likely be ignored. The final "punch," so to speak. Maybe this is why I procrastinate in finishing it and when I do, will I have the courage to send it?

Depositions are next week...do I wait until afterwards? Do I send him something before or does that make me more vulnerable? I can't stop thinking about him. Bottom line is, I'm not sure I'll ever completely "give up" on Matt. My prayer is for mutual forgiveness. Time, courage, humility. This is what is needed now.

You have no idea how your perspective has helped me. I have great anticipation when I log onto FB hoping to find a message from you. This is somewhat selfish because your writings inspire and bring me peace and comfort. Even through your struggles, I learn as I read about how you cope, how you process, how you respond. Mainly how you work through it and come out where you need and want to be. It's all extremely motivating and healing.

I've told a couple of people in my life about this literary journey we're on; my sisters and one of my dearest friends. I don't tell others for a couple of reasons, first, because I'm not sure they'd get it, and second, it's just odd I'd be in a helpful exchange with a famous comedian. But the people that I do tell, I always talk about the inner peace I feel when writing you. They are so very gratified, now, to understand that I have another genuine source of support in working through a difficult time in my life. So am I.

Craig Shoemaker   3/29, 8:39pm

I am not a comic who likes to be "on" all the time. I know people expect it of me but the obnoxious ones are the goof balls that command it. I always ask what they do for a living. If it is say…a nurse…I will say: "Okay, you want me to do my job on a day off? You do your job then. Give me an enema."

Was thinking about you and I do think you should finish that letter. Do it for you, not for him. Stand in your own integrity. You had 30 years to develop and love the way he wanted. You have tried to solicit what you want from Matt ad infinitum. Join me in taking the bold and courageous steps to let go of the old concepts to make room for what you deserve. Greatness takes great risk and there is nothing short of amazing rewards in order for you. The familiar is a breeding ground for resentment, which is a killer. Time to clean house, baby!

Leah De Luca   3/30, 8:03pm

Two big things I wanted to share with you. First, the latest round with the attorneys. In my last communication to Matt through his attorney, I asked that we resume communicating in whatever form Matt felt comfortable with. The response came back today from his attorney that "the client does not wish to communicate with your client in any fashion other than through the attorneys." So there you go. Secondly, you suggested to me that I finish the letter to Matt and "stand in my own integrity." What great advice Craig. I am feeling immense relief and inner freedom at this moment because I just hit the send button on an email message to Matt. It was a pretty simple message. I apologized for any pain I caused him and my need to express my "truths" during this process. I detailed my sadness over his unwillingness to communicate on any level and extended my forgiveness to him regarding the hurt I continue to feel. I basically ended it by telling him that I send him my love and that I hope one day we can both reach a place of grace and peace. I know he may never read or respond to it, but I have to tell you, I feel like a burden is lifted. While I will admit I am nowhere near cleaning house yet, I have gathered all the supplies needed and am ready to start dusting! Deep cleaning awaits me.

Craig Shoemaker   3/30, 9:28pm

I have a toothy grin reading your words. Whenever I witness positive metamorphosis, it makes me feel so human and alive. To evolve is such an undervalued, under-spoken action. We hear so much news that describes devolution, involving killing or disgraceful acts, but so little about some-one's growth. Damnation aplenty – salvation scarce.

Hearing about your action hits my heart. I feel like I was right there with you pressing the "send" button, feeling the emotional freedom right along with you. I am humbled but proud of you at the same time. The armistice you set into motion will do you a world of goodness.

You see, it is not about Matt anymore. This is exclusive to you and your journey. Your actions set into motion a clean space for you to operate from, and that is extraordinary. I am so happy you took the route of taking responsibility for your role in this drama. Another epidemic I believe destroys our world is the tendency to blame and build a case against the opposition.

My suspicion is that Matt will not respond. I don't think most folks comprehend forgiveness or apology. Actually, in my case, I've seen it used against me, as the attacker perceives a victory. Too bad for them. If they only knew the ecstasy one derives from letting go. Congratulations!

Leah De Luca   4/2, 7:38am

As it seems to be for you, these exchanges are a kind of therapy for me. Not just because of the inevitable relief they bring in being able to express myself, the good and bad, to someone who is neutral and nonjudgmental, but also because of witnessing the beauty of your daily journey, the highs, the lows, and all that lies in-between. To be honest, I now realize that I have never really known a man on any deep level, certainly not Matt, and it does make me feel sad to realize how much I have been missing. My deepest connections have been primarily with the women who are very close to me in my life, and to some extent my kids.

I wonder if my view of men is askew because in all the years I had with Matt, I really never came to know what his inner struggles were and how they affected who he is. We rarely talked about anything deep, and I think I really needed that to feel fully connected to him. I quickly gave up on having that critical aspect of what is a good relationship, because right or wrong, my experience with him taught me that he wasn't capable of providing that. It was very hard to get him to open up to me, and therefore me to him... though I desperately wanted to do just that. And this became my normal. I perpetuated a relationship for a lot of the wrong reasons.

I think I mentioned before that I once confided to a close friend that I yearned for a deeper personal and more intellectual connection with Matt. She reminded me to look at what Matt brought to the relationship rather than what he didn't. She thought I should realize that no one person can fulfill all of someone's needs and that I should look for other healthy and honorable outlets to fulfill those needs. Now, looking back, I think that this wasn't the best advice for me, primarily because the spiritual and intellectual connection I desired was so critically important to me. I needed to have it, at least some part of it, with my life's partner. I feel like I sold out. I definitely settled and certainly, I must not have been the woman I could have been to Matt, or what Matt needed, with my inner spirit being so unfulfilled.

Part of my journey is coming to understand what a relationship with a man "can be." I have the most amazing friendships, yet, I wanted that special connection with Matt. I now realize that I gave up on ever having it and along the way, lost sight of what "could be." Going back to you and what I glean from your relationship with Mika, I am thirsty for that. It's the kind of relationship that I hope to attract one day.

Craig Shoemaker   4/2, 1:13pm

I assure you, with the new space you are creating, the attraction of a man of substance and depth is already forming.

So excited today. About to watch the Phillies' opening game of the season. The first game has always been a huge day for me, since I was a little boy. I spent hours upon hours designing various lineups I felt would help my lowly Phils catapult to first place.

On opening day, no one is in first place. It's all even. Sure, there are some teams predicted to win it all, with just as many prognosticators talking about who will be mired in the cellar, yet on opening day, it means nothing. In the 70s, no matter how bad we looked on paper or what place we were in the year before, I was buoyantly confident. No one could shake my feelings about my home team. Call it blind optimism, however, nothing shook me from my position of full belief in my players.

We were poor, so couldn't afford good seats. I sat so high up in the 700 level, the hovering blimp was only feet away from scraping my head. But that didn't prevent me from truly believing that I was going to catch a fly ball. I patted my glove with every pitch as if I was a 10th fielder. The only break I took was when the slightly built, choke-up-on-the-bat Larry Bowa came to the plate, because I knew his limited power would never reach me in the upper deck. At Veteran's Stadium, if you caught a foul ball in the air, a graphic came up on the large scoreboard, which read, "Sign him up!" The stadium employee closest to the feat gave the sure-handed fan a pro-contract and supposedly an invite to try out for the team. This was the chance for my athletic talents to be noticed! I'm still waiting to snag a foul ball. Envious of batboys and vendors, I wanted to be on that field, or at least, closer to it. I figured that if I met a player, he'd secure me the job. Additionally, if they saw my physical prowess combined with locker room humor, I'd be a shoo-in!

After each game, I waited outside the stadium until the last janitor was gone, always with autograph pen and paper in hand. In the end, not only did I not get recognized for my hidden talents but Greg Luzinski tried to run me over with his car in the parking lot when I hounded him to sign a ball! My pen was never used to ink my name on a contract to be the 1976 Phanatic mascot, either. However, my biggest disappointment arose during my search for a father, as well as a husband for my heartbroken mother, whose opinion of men led me to believe she just needed a good guy to be with. I figured that would turn around her constant expressions of anger at the situation we were in. The most expressed reason for her misery being my dad's lack of child support payments.

I scanned every baseball card I owned for statistics. Sure, the home runs and stolen bases were important, but the key info I was looking for was an "s," which stood for "single," as in marital status. Not of the base-hit variety, but the bachelor kind. Yes, I wanted to fix my mom up with a husband, both to make her happy and to give me a guy to have a catch with!

I wrote a letter to Tim McCarver, the good looking and popular catcher for my Phightin' Phils, and sent it to Veteran's Stadium. Certainly, he needed a stepson to warm him up, right? I pictured us having a catch in the back yard of a home that was paid for, and him giving me tips on how to be a better ball player and man. I stamped the letter with great hope and anticipation, even sticking a pic of my mom in the envelope.

He never did write me back, but years later, I told my dad-quest story to his current broadcast partner, Joe Buck, whom I hung out with after my show. After hearing of the visions I had as a little boy, Joe had his partner inscribe a baseball for me. It's my most wonderful prized possession. Written on the ball: "Dear Son; Time to grow up! Love, Dad. aka, Tim McCarver."

Some good things you just have to wait for. In due time my "father" finally appeared by written advice on a ball...but my dream "Pops" still hasn't taught me how to throw a curve! BTW, I still haven't met Tim. Perhaps I will keep him as just my imagination.

I guess my childish enthusiasm, combined with a tendency to harbor unrealistic expectations, still exists with me as an adult. When I married my ex-wife, I submitted a lineup that was a positive winner. On paper, look out! From what I saw, she was a can't-miss prospect, a seasoned veteran, but had never had her shot at the Major Leagues (marriage and motherhood), and I was the man to give her that chance. What I did not foresee was that the potential was a far departure from what was observed with my untrained eye. The reasons she had not succeeded at career, education, relationships or love, were also some key reasons why our marriage failed. The entitled way she conducts her life, thinking she is "owed" and we are her loyal subjects, reminds me of the failed athletes that do not live up to their scouting reports. Ability aplenty but no commitment or sacrifice, which it takes to win, and no accountability either. My lack of scrutiny and proper appraisal has bitten me in the ass – a lot. I want immediate payoff, the victory and attention. However, I many times in the past didn't want to go through the uncomfortable rigors of practice...I want to be in the game - NOW.

My avoidance of perspiration has led to unnerving exasperation. Mental illness is a bitch, figuratively and in this case, literally. Major League bummer right now is that this hellcats' disease is back in full swing. It is scary, frustrating and daunting. Over the past month, she has been on a level-10 assault mode. At first, her sights were on Mika. Currently, she is affecting all. In war they call it "collateral damage." My poor business manager, Liz, Debby reams her too, accusing her of fraud and all else. The ex screams at Liz, telling her she's a sexist and an accessory to a child molester because of her collusion with me. I'm sure she's thinking: "This crap ain't worth 5 percent"...of my now dwindled income!

I used to have no understanding about what kind of patience and diligence was required to be successful, not only in career, but in relationships of all kinds. Albeit in a different form, when I fail, it's not too far from Debby's protocol of not thinking things through, acting on impulse and responding from emotion.

I am that, I am.

Yesterday indicated we are a little closer to the past I thought had passed. I received a cc email from a mom (friend of mine), who wrote to Debby with tremendous concern and upset. Apparently, this mother had been cornered (common with my ex) and got an earful she did not invite or expect. In the schoolyard pickup area, Debby yells out of seemingly nowhere to anyone listening, "I'm a good mother! Whatever my ex says about me is a lie. I know you're friends with him but I want to warn you he's a sociopath! He will lure you in and hurt you like he does everyone. Craig is sick. He showed Michael videos of anal penetration when my son was 7! I have the court papers to prove it. We are going back to court. He has Mika write letters for him and they won't stop harassing me. They want to fight and I have lawyers. He is sick and I am telling you to watch out. I am a wonderful mother!" She screamed this in front of first-graders, the teacher, four parents and other little boys within earshot. When that temper of hers flares, nothing stops the missile launch. Game on! It is a state of unconsciousness. It is a win-at-all-costs force that cannot be reckoned or reasoned with. Hey, maybe she would make a good ball player?? When one is on the wrong end of this kind of tirade, it is beyond comprehension. One cannot reason with her or find logic in what she is rambling about. It is emotion like a bullet, flying through the air without the slightest interruption or impediment, an eruption where you just get out of the way.

One asset or problem I have is: no backing down. I'm the type of guy who believed I could do a surface dive through a tidal wave. No exaggeration. I actually was down with the tsunami if it dared to strike the Jersey Shore. If we were in the middle of a flash flood, I'd be the last guy to evacuate. I'll be the hero and save our home and all who occupy it. Through logic, reason and cunning, I can solve this difficult situation. Leave it to me, the starting Phillies left fielder, matchmaker and part-time pro mascot, to deliver us from this evil. Well, that is a me I am leaving behind. If personal growth is a telethon tote board and a thousand is the tops, I'm at about an 850.

Leah De Luca   4/2, 7:38pm

Craig, it's so hard to comprehend what was going on in the mind of your ex. I think you hit it with the mental illness. The portion of your letter that rang loud and clear was when you wrote; "When one is on the wrong end of this kind of tirade, it is beyond comprehension. I cannot reason with her or find logic in what she does. Like a bullet, flying through the air without the slightest interruption or impediment, she is an eruption, where you just get out of the way and hope not to absorb too much damage." I can empathize. Reading the bits about who you were as a boy, your view of the world, about your favorite teams and players, your mom, yourself and what you wanted for you, for her… man….love it. Tells quite the story of innocence, love, disappointment, courage, anticipation, fear, humor (loved that the note finally got to McCarver!)…the whole gamut.

The symbolism between the ideas of having a potentially winning team and line up, and what you thought Debby could be to you or become, is pretty enlightening. You talk about seeing her with the "untrained" eye and how that has come full circle in your life. I feel so similarly about Matt, yet to some extent, I knew exactly what I was getting into. Back to you though…I can tell you that I know EXACTLY what you are talking about. And you actually have to LIVE through an experience like that to truly understand it. Trying to explain it in words, powerful as they may be, is an entirely different experience than witnessing it.

Craig Shoemaker 4/3, 11:25am

Been eatin' some feelings lately, and my enlarged belly is an "extension" of the rising amount of swallowing I've been doing. Now trying to shed a few pounds of buildup. Not at my goal weight, but on my way. I realize when I binge and eat the wrong things, it leads to some unwanted pounds and tiring easier too. I devour the worst possible food when I feel overwhelmed and caught in the trap of trying to change a Borderline. If I want to be "trim and fit," so to speak, I need to pay attention to self and give my body what it needs, not what I am addicted to. I was literally raised on poor people's food, with a non-recommended daily requirement of fats, bad carbs and sugars. My blood type is "Cherry."

When I don't pay careful mind to my soul, I order up a plate of conflict. I crave it, cuz I'm used to it. I might be enjoying a regular, normal day and then BOOM! I am beamed over to an all-you-can-eat, $1.99 buffet with the other cattle. I pile it on and don't even look up or take a breath. I was so used to things being in disarray when I was a child and onward, I now look for it if it's not even there. I actually open up email with frightening anticipation. "Will Debby write a note I can respond to with my clever retorts? Did she get back to me on the requests I've made? Will she be kind and reasonable, since I begged her to do so again? Will she finally write a single word of regret and remorse for all the harm she does, just to demonstrate she is normal beneath all the mayhem she causes?

Do I have similar thirst or suspense over searching/discovering an email that speaks of how much I am LOVED? Not too often...I keep a file called, "Divorce," filled with notes, exchanges and evaluations from many years of high conflict. Is there a file called, "Best marriage ever?" Well, there will be now. Be right back...

Ok, I'm back...

As much as I want to say Debby is sick, it is my illness that brought this latest giant pile of crap to our camp. Damn, she stirs the pot of shit, why do I always end up licking the spoon? I asked for it, that's why. No, not directly, but by indirect connection to the Big G, rather than being consistent in my quest for higher self. Similar to a passive prayer, where I continue to request the gifts from my youth, instead of asking for more of what I am already – pure love. The "familiar" is to set up a situation where there is unresolved conflict, even if I have to conjure some up in the moment, and once I do so, I can begin the process of fixing it. Instead of marinating myself in monumental soul purpose, I veer into ego-driven rescue mode, subconsciously figuring if I resolve the issues for all around me, I will finally be viewed as a good guy. To be the man with the plan gets me seen and heard, something terribly missing from my childhood and beyond. Maybe if McCarver had written me back sooner, none of this would be happening?!

Leah, I've been thinking…is writing your hidden passion? I wonder, is this going to be one of those stories of a woman trapped in a dead-end marriage, forgoing and putting away her dreams of being an author? Anyway, I had a revelation this morning and it makes me chuckle. I mean, here's a woman whom I've met casually a couple dozen times in public places with lots of people around, with a husband dominating all conversation, who is in the midst of a multi-page deep and revealing dialogue, with a man primarily known as a standup comic, who's finally found a happy marriage and lives 3000 miles away.

The entire Facebook private-message conversation was prompted by breakup of marriage and developed into a mixed bag of stories, anecdotes, discovery, secrets and advice. Two people, unrelated and virtual strangers, with no romantic or financial agenda, have come together in offering monumental support, which they both yearned for and needed. A man and a woman who grew up in vastly different circumstances, but both spending decades eschewing what was good for them so they could make others happy. MOST would say this is NUTS. It is supposed to be family or at least a close friend who supplies these kinds of outlets, right? Most people are run by fear and ignorance. They dare not to take a breath to examine the multiple dimensions in front of them. I have numerous thoughts on this but I have to take a nap. Maybe when I wake up, there will be a new "chapter" coming from the new American novelist in my in-box??

Craig Shoemaker   4/3, 3:30pm

Waiting with baited breath…in the meantime; I'm Googling the origin/meaning of "baited breath."

Craig Shoemaker

Gotta tell ya, your new friend Craig must not be headed to the ethereal gym much, because I am attracting some ugly of late. In this latest drama, I will be honest. I need to rise to forgiveness. Although my ex is certainly very disturbed, who am I to judge the level of sickness? To make her the identified patient will get me nowhere either – maybe backwards, but nothing with forward motion. My errors are aplenty here. Mostly, I was the one who needled the beast and didn't expect it to roar. I don't do these things intentionally. Unearthing this as I write. Might not do things to the degree she does but that does not diminish my function in this latest unrest.

If I kept an eye exclusively on myself, this would not have taken place. What I did in this sequence was begin it by basically telling Debby she should have handled Johnny's doctor visit better. Mika wrote the letter at my prompting, telling Debby what the doctor had advised her and that we should always arrange a time with him – not go to urgent care, who misdiagnosed and wrongly prescribed Johnny's illness.

Actually, I did another thing that has led to lifetime trouble too – called her on one of her lies. Have had a few pathological liars in my life, and the general common element in all is how they protect their image with all they have. If someone else outside the circle sees something they shouldn't, then an all-out effort is made to cover up. Obviously this includes either non-truths or running away. Reverse accusation also goes on – anything to take it away from honesty. When this dominant ball of righteous energy is formed, I should get the hell out of the way. But nope. Little Craigy fights for truth and justice.

The only balance I will ever find is internal. Funny (not!) that I was married to someone so OFF-balanced but guess that was the plan for me. One lesson to learn is not to approach a heart & soul problem with intellect, reason or practicality. Relief will not be found by figuring it out. Only by taking bold and diligent action of undiluted purpose will we get where we need to be.

I created this. One way I fell from grace is that I started to launch passive-aggressive verbal jabs about Debby to Michael. I disguised it as caring for the family, but nothing good will come out of involving the kids. Whatsoever. Plus, it is something I accuse her of and deplore in her (letting kids in on it), but here I am doing the same thing. I'm angry that she allowed Johnny to hear her screaming about me, and here I am causing the yells by basically teasing it out of her.

Giving this deeper contemplation. Had better nip this bitterness in the bud. I hate her, but need to move to a better place with that or suffer the fate of a man steeped in resentment.

This is old me versus new me. I used to imagine sports fans chanting, "Shoe! Shoe! Shoe!" Now hoping for imaginary friends in my head to yell "New! New! New!" Let's give it up for new Shoe. The refreshed one is going to apologize, mostly by amending my behavior. Something has been compelling me to be magnetically moved to a higher force, and that is certainly the case now.

 Craig Shoemaker   4/5, 11:40 pm

Once I wrote this, wow! What an escape from miserable self-pity. Got to lift my innards by spilling to you, prompting me to take action I would not have, if not for coming clean. This uncovering is working for me! It also leads to the kids having a better dad and Mika having a less irritated husband. Right after closing out my letter to you, I Skyped Mika and Jackson from my hotel room in Tampa. Feeling unchained, I was clowning with them and having a blast when suddenly, unexpectedly, Michael came into the room. He is with his mom this weekend, but stopped by to hang with his step-mom and little brother.

I gently asked him to come closer to the laptop camera. I easily and gracefully apologized for putting him in the middle of his mom and me. He was reticent at first, but then a sense of calm seemed to come over him once he saw where I was coming from. "I thought you were going to be mad at me, Dad," he said, apparently knowing about the rift going on from his mom's camp. She bullies and is so insistent that I am an ogre who is destroying his life. She tries to convince him that his good feelings about me are not real, that her views are the appropriate and more accurate. How confused this boy must be. Once he saw I was not reacting the way she had predicted, he started to unveil some personal angst he was feeling. I kept on point with how I regretted telling him to give a message to Debby about picking up Johnny late each day. "Tell your mom if she is running late that me or Mika will assist if she asks." That is simply not the way to engage with someone of her ilk. Him telling her what I asked was what inflamed her, leading to the schoolyard rant.

I assuaged Michael's fears and made it clear that my actions were not in good faith and that I'd do my very best not to do such a thing in the future. He felt obvious relief and comfort, and expressed his frustrations with his mom. "Mom owes me an apology more than you do." I knew what he meant, that she blew this thing up as she frequently does, which is probably another reason he made an impromptu visit to our home, getting away from the craziness of Casa de Debby. I stayed on track with keeping the microscope on me, asking that he listen to me and forget his issues with his mom for the time being. "Michael, this is important that you hear what I am saying. Your mom is not here now and has nothing to do with this. I want you to know how much I love you and how sorry I am that I involved you."

He thanked me and said he heard what I was saying. He got it. To see his freedom was a delight. I was elevated and walked around so happy, practically skipping to work across the outdoor mall. So, even though you haven't written back about any of this, it is the knowing you are an ally and great recipient of my catharsis. I fully trust you. What a great thing that is for me. You are a goodsend.

Leah De Luca   4/6, 7:34pm

Crap! I wanted to begin writing you around 1am and knew that if I started, I'd be up a long time. As it seems to be for you, these exchanges are a kind of therapy for me. And not just because of the inevitable relief they bring in being able to express myself, the good and bad, to someone who is neutral and nonjudgmental, but also because of witnessing the beauty of your daily (ok, sometimes weekly) journey, the highs, the lows, and all that lies in-between. The feeling of joy in watching you work through every challenge and coming always back to your true self, is so gratifying. And selfishly, I yearn for your stories of past and present as well (not that I wish that you would go through anything difficult), because I learn so much. I love your honesty, your openness, your ability to express EXACTLY what you are feeling, and your strong desire to evaluate situations and the people in your life from every vantage point.

I think this is why Mika, now having been directly involved recently, more clearly understands what mental issues can do to a person, even herself. And in those moments of the kind of "eruption" you speak of – that is when you completely give up trying. It's when you do, in fact, "get out of the way." For anyone whose purpose is to be enlightened, informed, fair, honest, it's just simply no match. When you realize that you are outmatched by that kind of insanity, it's almost as if you are on the personal precipice of complete calm and peace. Giving in, not to the perpetrator, but to yourself, when reaching the fiercest part of the storm, is when inner peace is resurrected…it's when you reach the eye of the storm and when the chaos ends…at least for the moment.

It has to be hard as hell to be wondering what she is up to now, with the rants in the schoolyard and the threats of lawyers, etc. I can see why you literally have to consciously work through what's happened, what's happening, and what's to come. The irony of the incident at school is the insecure rants of the kind of mother she is, yet, the example she set for her son and others is the antithesis of her goal. As a dad, I imagine the hardest part for you has to be in wanting to protect your sons. I see that you sympathize with what they go through. They are innocent bystanders, their minds and souls ripe for influence. And that is why I love what you do every day. I love that you opened up to Michael and apologized for your part. One of your best attributes is your utter determination to show your sons what "should be." The older they get, the more they will realize this. And clearly, Michael is already yearning for more time in that "balanced" place that is your home with Mika. He is being attracted there, for all the right reasons. And while Michael, more than anyone, may be the one who struggles with all of this, he has a gift in having you as his dad…no matter what missteps you may make along the way.

Still writing! Got sidetracked by a phone call…whew! This feels good…

My phone won't stop ringing! Sorry…clearly, writing at 1am will have to be preferred going forward because you don't get interrupted. Anyway, you know, something hit me in reading about your role in needling the giant…I have to tell you that while I truly admire (and try to emulate) this kind of process, I think sometimes we also need to be called on the carpet for what is NOT our doing. In your case, you speak of questioning Debby about the way in which she went about handling the urgent care visit as something that needled her into her usual aggression.

I don't know Craig, I'm not sure if I totally buy that one. While I agree on the basis of fact that it may have caused her to go on her mission of drama, I also believe that as a parent, you have every right and responsibility to weigh in on matters such as these. Is it possible that people who are co-parenting but doing it separately can have very different philosophies on matters of health, education, etc. when it comes to their kids...and can avoid conflict? Not likely. Knowing you, I imagine you would like nothing more than to have some kind of agreement memorialized about how you will agree to parent on a day-to-day basis to avoid the kind of chaos that is your ex. That said, how do you do that when you have someone questioning your writing in the little box in the homework folder? Here I am, talking myself through some of what you probably do continually. So now, I again see the methods to your madness! Your process of confronting, addressing, releasing, and working through to higher ground may, in fact, be a continual process that is necessary for the kind of outcome you require. So I applaud you and if I can be nothing more than a sounding board (I feel like a guy...I desperately want to solve the problems...but really just need to be here to listen)...I am extremely grateful and honored to have that role.

Craig Shoemaker   4/7, 9:30am

Today, your role is author. What you just transcribed was as moving as any book I've read. It hit me hard. Strangely, like Debby's bullet, your love, kindness and compassion flew into me without hesitation or obstacle changing its flight. My guy-head clutter can usually stop something like that from getting through but in this case, my protector shield was down and my emotional fortress got penetrated. I peeked to see that you had written me and almost paused my movie to read. Glad I didn't because it allowed you to finish your thought. Yes, old me wanted to get in the game but new me is glad I delayed gratification. What's with the "he who hesitates is lost?" Who wrote that – a hyena? Like, unless you pounce and devour the first thing that comes along, you will lose out on the meal.

Well, here's my return quote – "pause for the cause." If the cause is inner Shangri-La, then take a moment to reflect on an alternative route to getting there. Take a break from what is seemingly natural to the hunters & gatherers – to survive by being the strongest and fastest, so one can be better equipped to put more food on the table. But, there are many in the animal kingdom who seem to be the most evolved, who use a different style of getting their needs met, through cunning and guile, patiently sussing out the situation and their prey, leading to sharp, instinctual prowess. You can tell by the body language of wild animals which of the beasts is confident and in charge and who are the desperate, greedy and needy. It's almost as if the other primates and cats live a better life in the jungle, commanding respect through their confident exuding of intelligence, critical thought and staying in the moment; whereas many others, like vultures, leeches and jackals, are visibly ugly, and miserable in their existence as those who rely on others to do the work for them.

Leah, sometimes what you write overwhelms me to the point where I stop my brain and let the feelings take over. I let it be and real emotions are the result. Your wordswomanship is so good, I went right back to read it again, where I was able to take in more sensory morsels I had not consumed the first go-through.

Twas contemplating the root of my touched feelings. What I immediately identified was how good it felt to be acknowledged. To be seen for the man I am and want to be is rare. To add, when you say some things you say, it feels as if someone is protecting me, and that is a lifelong quest. I have been found at the well with an empty bucket all too many times. You know, part of what I'm finding in all this is this -- there are human written "laws" we are run by but upon further review, most are useless and serve no fulfilling purpose.

One old piece of thinking is about family. Here is my family of origin; on paper the very backbone of my character. "Blood is thicker than water," (another quote to investigate) we've heard ad infinitum; yet many times find the converse. My family of origin does not have the spiritual riches to share with others. Worse, they don't want to even discuss taking the path of perceptively most resistance. To choose to rise above the generations of using the template handed to us, hence redesigning a new way of existing, is where I want to be. In the case of Craig & Leah, if you submitted the case to a court of public opinion, our bonding interrelation should not exist, especially to the degree that it does.

Oh, by the way, it is not "baited breath." That would mean putting worms or squid in your mouth and waiting for a fish to come. It's actually "bated breath." It comes from "abated." Spiritus = breath. Bated breath = soothe, calm, toned down... It is something I cannot hear enough. Researching that term's origin brought me there AGAIN. Ok, Mr. Man Upstairs, I get it!! Gotta take a nap. Maybe when I wake up, it will to a new "chapter" coming from the great new novelist of this century??

Leah De Luca   4/8, 2:08pm

I have to get my game on before I write to you so that I can measure up. I do enjoy writing, but never thought about it much.

Funny, I had a conversation with my boss the other day. He was getting ready for an interview for another position and he asked me to challenge him with questions I thought he might be asked. We did this for a while and then I asked him what his greatest "personal" challenge would be if he were offered and accepted the position. This threw him off because usually you're asked about what kinds of challenges you'd foresee about the position or the organization, but not the personal challenges.

He talked about managing his diabetes and how it had impacted him throughout these many past years and how it never stopped him from reaching his goals. He talked about the compassion he has for people because of his plight and why that makes him a better leader. Then the tables turned and he started asking me questions! Wait! I'm not the one going for a job! However, I played along. He asked me, "What do you do to 'create' in your personal life?" This one stumped me...and that bothered me. I defaulted to rambling on about what joy I have being a mom. I threw in cooking. Clearly I didn't answer the question, at least not how I wanted to. And I love it because this made me think hard about what it is I desire to create. I've been thinking about that conversation ever since. Maybe you've inspired me to look into writing as a possible way to create. Who knows! :)

Heading out in a little bit with friends but this is getting to be an addiction (of a good sort). I will write again tomorrow but all I want to say for now, is that it's good to let your emotions flow. Tears are truly a gift. They cleanse the soul. It's such a pure and spiritual form of releasing. A good cry is like great sex with the person you love, you feel exhausted and yet reinvigorated all at the same time, and in the most amazing way. It clears the slate for a new way of thinking or behaving and resets the soul to where it needs to be. By the way, if you continue to be in touch with your emotions, I highly recommend crying in the shower. I don't really know why, and if you haven't tried it, laughing through tears is actually my ALL-time favorite emotion!

Thankful that I found an unlikely friendship in you. You came at exactly the right time in my life and brought something to my soul that no one else could. I am CONVINCED that a higher power brought you to me. Thank you, from my heart.

CHAPTER SEVEN

GETTING PAST THE PAST

Craig Shoemaker 4/9, 11:13pm

Just wrapped up a long weekend in Fort Lauderdale. The shows have been stellar of late, as I near the filming of my 90-minute standup comedy special for SHOWTIME on Friday. I'm approaching this shoot with more dedication than any endeavor I've taken on before; doing things that will have me fully prepared. I'm actually working out! I used to have a joke in my act that was very true: "I work out once a year. January 2nd, when I join a new health club."

Yes, for my New Year's Resolution I'd sign a year-contract at a fancy fitness club, then put too much into pleasing my assigned trainer. Typical for me, I'd overdo it, thinking to myself that she will say, "Wow, you're so strong. You sure you don't work out?" I wanted to not only be the best beginner she ever saw, but her phone number too. But then my muscles were sore, the recovery time took long…so I'd just quit going to the club instead of starting all over from scratch. My tight abs atrophied – end of program till the next winter. As is customary for me, I keep relying on natural talent and skill and sometimes get a little lazy. There's an underlying thought that I'm somewhat afraid of what indeed will happen when I give it all I have, where I will be seen as never before and be subjected to mass judgment and criticism. Like I'll be "found out" as a fraud and exposed.

I have been at this comedy thing for a lifetime, starting when I was a teenager, getting up on stage whenever and wherever I could. But I wasn't being real back then, instead, I took safe roads when writing material, not jumping in with all I have. I took an avenue where I could play the game but not the big one, hanging out at a distance from the great comics who took risks and delved deeper into their work. Now, I am finally ready. I think it's due to having breakthroughs in matters such as this; peeling away the residue of a life in hiding – I now am very clear on my purpose and who I am in this world. For many years, I relied on doing impressions and characters. One time in the late 90s my manager said, "You know, Craig, Hollywood doesn't know your point of view. You need to show them what you are and write material that is uniquely yours."

I argued, defending my position, telling him, "What if my point of view is that I don't have one, that my impressions are a way of wearing a mask?" I began my rants of listing the comics who had no point of view and then I'd spit out resentments regarding the jackasses running show biz. I'm sure you can see how far I got with that bitter stance!

When I realized that [the beat I was following] led to little progress, I started to heed the advice from my former manager, developing my point of view.

The more I realized that honesty and self-evaluation would lead to a better life, my career and art reached another level. Now, on stage and off, my confidence is at its highest. Not in a cocky way, but the opposite, I turned my will over to the source of absoluteness, integrity and profound inner freedom. Unity with goodness lead the way to my discovery of the authentic me.

Parents mean well, and many times give you what they were instructed to do by their caretakers. Mostly, the customs, mores, values and morals are what are passed to the next generation. In my case, the prevailing message I received was to not rock the boat. Don't bother anyone. Make sure secrets stay secret.

Maybe I wrote this before, but my kidnap/molestation moment when I was thirteen is very telling as to how my family functioned. Without being honest about the issues of great significance, the lie of omission poisons us. In order to deal with my emotions, I developed the tendency to blame others and justify. Run from the truth. Never apologize, because apologies imply defeat. This was the death of my true self; the real man I spent years trying to avoid. This was the example my parents gave me.

Yet, as life would have it, the supposedly wonderful world I wanted others to believe would eventually be found out. If I didn't have the answers, I pretended to. When my vulner-abilities were jeopardized, others would take me down...or so I falsely believed.

The protection of our lies was paramount in our family. When I was told not to tell anyone of my horrific weekend at the hands of a serial sexual predator, it threw me for a loop. Our life screenplay did not contain moral reasoning. It was craziness, but I learned to play the part and formed my identity on the quicksand of backwards values. Like my mom,

CRAIG SHOEMAKER

grandmother and most others in our clan, I pointed fingers at anyone who did not fall in line with what I thought was the way all should be. I often thought: "Why don't they get it?"

I cannot begin to express how important it is to remain steady in living humbly and gratefully. In humility, truth exists. I now recognize that I am human. It is so transformative to live in the certainty of knowing that I will be okay no matter what illusions of obstacles may appear. When I get out of the way and let universal order take over, astonishing things take place. Relating this to the divorce mess, I can see that this "new thinking" really works. Defensive, fear-based actions do not. With faith in good outcome beyond my limited thinking, the conclusion is inevitably a great one. Once I stopped playing out what was dictated to me by my family, I was able to create a better destiny. Where I previously found myself in repetitive sequels, I now enjoy an original production with a happy, exciting and promising ending.

Leah, even though you might not see it, the best is yet to come. But only if you throw out the screenplay and create one that has not yet been written. When connected with The Big G as the co-writer, it is a far better and richer epic. Become the star, not the supporting character in someone else's hackneyed story! It takes tremendous trust. We must lay down our arms. When it's perceived that our exes will gain something from their disgusting actions, the tendency is to fight for our "rights." There is only one "right," the higher variety kind. When lawyers run the show, they abandon a heaven-on-earth plan. Attorneys have no interest in something ethereal. Their goal is to win, and they will do so any way possible. What I discovered is that the more I resist fighting on their terms, the more I actually "win" on mine. Think about what you are fighting for prior to responding to his lawyers. Contemplate what you want on a prayerful level. If you want freedom, then do what it takes to gain that. Every time you submit a problem you find in Matt, is another chance for him to defend. When that takes place, you have already seen how that works. You lob an arrow; he sends a Scud.

If you remain wrapped up in old ways of thinking, you fail to recognize the love you deserve, hence, delaying personal fulfillment and happy destiny. I am reminded of the biblical quote, "The meek shall inherit the earth." How true, yet habitually we have come to think the opposite; that there is power in money and control. You have no power over Matt's behavior. Yet you have control over your own actions, particularly the ones that have delivered years of misery.

Leah De Luca   4/10, 5:34am

Thank you, thank you! Needed this before work. This reinforces what deep down I know is the right way to go. Exactly what I wanted to hear. Back later.

Craig Shoemaker   4/10, 8:50am

"Exactly what I wanted to hear..." It is such a comfort to me to know that people like you are out there. Isn't it staggering to travel through these isolated spots, where not many have trampled on the natural beauty? Isn't this rarified air so sweet? I like to visit these exotic and beautiful places of uncommon delight. Sure beats meeting at the strip mall. Now, if there were about 10 million more of you, maybe I could write a book?!

Thought of a new term, "whynamics." It's the dynamic of questioning "why," instead of reacting in ways that have previously led to bad fortune. Whynamics remind us to keep close to the purpose of soaring, hence moving away from the handed-down messages that make you into a version of self that will never be satisfied.

Leah De Luca   4/11, 8:16pm

Warning...this isn't going to be the most moving of our Facebook chronicles. Some of this is old news however; I need to hash it out. I appreciate your acknowledgement of the things and feelings that could be holding me back. It amazes me that it doesn't really matter how dissimilar our stories are, because I feel you understand what I'm dealing with.

So, the communications between our attorneys over the past several months have been absent of my hurling anything at Matt. I actually took care of any and all the hurling in my counterclaim for divorce months ago. However, I made a giant error in judgment by basically saying three things in my counterclaim: 1) *He was unfaithful to me.* To this day I don't know exactly how or all the facts. No matter, because I eventually lost respect for him. And in time, I lost respect for me, because I allowed myself to continue in a pattern of dysfunction. Over time it became less about whatever constituted this "unfaithfulness," than it was coming face to face with the reality of my situation. I felt so trapped in not being able to make things right. 2) *He abused alcohol.* This led to many an argument, hurt feelings, misunderstandings, and a cycle of hurt during the marriage, at least for me. 3) *He made some financial decisions without my prior knowledge.* That's it. Not pretty, but true. True for me, that is. He in turn denied most of these allegations. Bottom line though, these "grounds" can never portray what occurred throughout a 30-year marriage, can they? And certainly if you were having this exchange with him, he might see things very differently but in a cumulative way, I felt that this is what brought me to my own breaking point.

In my heart I believe that Matt was torn-up with guilt or sadness, over the things that brought me to my own breaking point. I believed him when he said he still loved me and wanted to keep our marriage together. However this time, and for the first time, it was me who was behaving selfishly and in my own self-interest. I honestly just couldn't live this way anymore. It was enough for me. Just enough. Yet some part of me still loves this man very, very much. It feels like an emotional roller coaster at times. As I look deeper, I can now say that the grounds I filed in my counterclaim really weren't grounds at all. They were more symptoms, as I perceived them, and not the real "cause" or "grounds" for my present actions. Perhaps the real grounds should have been eroded trust and respect, failure to grow as a couple, and lack of any basic foundation of a strong and spiritual relationship – grounds that we were both clearly guilty of.

Regardless, I have been feeling guilty about the counterclaim, hence, my recent apology e-mail to Matt. I didn't apologize to end his fury, though that would be a wonderful side benefit. Instead, I apologized because I AM, genuinely sorry. I didn't lie, but my honesty certainly tore him apart. Hurting Matt is a very new concept for me. I spent 30 years trying NOT to hurt him, at my own expense, yet, in the past 6-7 months I have probably hurt him more than I have in our entire marriage. Not proud of that. I have never betrayed my own true self more than I did in four short months. A shift in my perspective in recent months does in fact have a lot to do with what I've learned from you.

The only thing left to fight over is finances. The most recent communications revolve around trying to get Matt to be honest about his sources of income. Conversely, Matt's communications have been very attacking in nature. I unfortunately feel I have to defend myself but I do not return with counterattacks. I am beginning to realize and accept that Matt has no intention of being honest. The thing that bothers me the MOST about all of this is the dishonesty and how he uses lies for his personal gain. I'm a fair person. I don't get caught up in a battle for a battle's sake, but it's really hard for me to give up on honesty and to swallow a settlement that is based on untruths. Perhaps truth looks different to different people, including me.

At one point, I felt a much stronger will to "fight" than I do now, if not for me, than for our kids. The kids will be ok. I will be ok. I desperately want to put this chapter behind me. And I can't tell you how much I want to explore the person I want to be, the person I'm destined to be but never "got out of my OWN way" to find. I'm getting there. Slowly...but surely.

By the way, congratulations on the upcoming filming of your special. One of the many things I admire about you is your ability to use your journey to inner self and apply it in every single aspect and role in your life. Not only did letting go bring you to Mika but it brought you to even greater success in your professional life. It's as if you can't miss – the more true to yourself you are, the "easier" it becomes to fulfill your destiny with the utmost of happiness and success. That isn't to intimate that any of it is "easy," rather the fulfillment just comes naturally.

One last, and the most important thing I want to acknowledge, is what happened to you years ago with the sexual molestation. I am pretty sure there isn't much I could ever say to make the hurt go away. Not just the hurt from the actual predator's acts but from the memory, and the fact that you had to pretend that it never happened. All I want to say is that my heart is with you on this. You are probably one of a very small number of people in this world who can come to grips with what happened and turn it around in a way that makes sense. I'm really honored to know you, not because you've been through something so terrible and survived, but because of your daily choice to confront your past and use it in the most wholesome way to continued inner growth. I want to apologize to you if I glossed over something so deeply hurtful that you expressed and got hung up on my own seemingly insignificant issues. I am here if you ever need to let more out on this. You are correct in saying that with no agenda whatsoever, it is very easy to be here for one another, and very healing.

Craig Shoemaker   4/12, 12:32am

I appreciate your kind words. I must tell you, that of all the abuse I have been a part of, it is not necessarily the actual crime committed that bothers me, as much as it is the lack of support I received from the people who were supposed to love me. To me, my mother's lack of concern regarding the molestation incident, and now her condoning my ex-wife's horrific acts against me and my family, is beyond comprehension. My mom and sister STILL are perpetrators of tremendous betrayal; befriending Debby, while completely cutting off me, Mika and Jackson. They even wrote disparaging notes to the family court about me! I guess I've adapted. I have this sense that I can get past anything with impassioned determination.

I became a grown-up too soon. Went right to the chameleon part, not addressing the painful issues that come along after one is roughed up. I skipped over the grieving and went right into survival mode. I keep thinking about my mother, going about her life in Philly, not once picking up the phone to ask how I'm doing or voicing her concern about the effects of the bitter divorce and ongoing assaults on my character. Actually, she still helps Debby in her quest to get me and has often been used in court docs to portray me in a bad light, all because I refuse play by her rules. This turning of her back hurts so much. 99.9% of the time I diminish the problem and ignore the pain, pretending to be okay about it, but I am not. I feign disconnection, when in fact I am deeply hitched to the feelings of abandonment and insecurity. I might want someone to notice or listen, but I stash that away fast.

I recalled today the many times when I was beaten up as a kid. One time, three boys in my neighborhood came into my house to get at me. I was a bit of a delinquent myself, but would never even think about going into a family home to beat someone up. Imagine the lack of family protection I had, if kids could force entry and beat up someone in their own home! These were the days where even using the word "bully" would get you even MORE bullying. We had just moved into another town and I had to switch schools to the rival Junior High, since we had been evicted yet again from the home before it. Stability was nonexistent in my lexicon, and this move was particularly chaotic and traumatic for me. I didn't fit in at this new school and I did all I could to find a crowd. Although I was the second smallest boy in our grade, I still went out for the football team. All the cool guys were on the team and they were good too. Desperately, I wanted the kinship and male bonding.

What I received was sheer terror. I chose a position no one wanted, one where I could be a part of the action – a center. A lineman is supposed to be the biggest in size. I was 5 feet and 77 pounds. I tried putting on some thick arm pads to disguise the lack of forearms. It wasn't the other team I needed to intimidate, but the players on our own. It didn't work. I did my best tough act. Nothing, I mean nothing, stopped these kids from literally pounding the shit out of me daily. Humiliation was their primary goal, and that included wedgies, where they pulled my white Fruit-of-the-Looms violently up my ass crack until it bled, leaving nothing but the elastic band. The locker room became a coyote wilding. I was the small animal they all wanted to devour.

I didn't want to burden my mom so I made up stories as to why my undie drawer was empty. I concocted lie after lie, along with telling her how awesome I was faring in football, knowing damn well she would never attend a game to verify. There would be no sticking up for me either, as she deemed most of what I said "complaining."

I made the starting lineup. We were a great team but if anything went wrong with an offensive play, I was blamed. The disdain and rage on our quarterback's face was beyond comprehension. In the huddle, he gave the play with the instructions on snap count. I was the first to be released to go set up the ball for the hike. He grabbed my facemask and smacked it with such force, yelling, "Good snap, asshole!"

We won every game, yet I was not a part of the celebration. They violently hit, kicked and punched me. I had no idea what to do about it. If I ran to the coach, surely I'd regret it and be beaten worse. My mother was not an audience either. Though very smart and full of answers, she would have none for me, as emotional ones would always stump her. As I had been so many times in the past, I was on my own. In many ways, the school of hard knocks was a good thing, spawning growth. However, on the other hand, I loathe what festered inside about my mom and dad, who still show no interest in my welfare or me. I sound whiny when I say this. I hate even writing it as I have developed such disdain for the victim mentality. And so, I'll end the self-pity here.

Today, I was challenged yet again by my ex-wife. In this recent provocation, she simply will not calm down or go away. No matter how many times we state what the court agreement says about no phone calls to our home, she does it anyway. With each call, she leaves a message, the kind where you can hear the anger seething and growing. She called three times within 40 minutes. This began to upset me. I did my best to turn my head because I knew if I answered I would be subjecting myself to more harassment. I am very much aware that if I pick it up, there goes any progress out the window. Mika said it's like training a dog. We must be firm in our dedication to improving the behavior and cannot give in. I said that if she writes a note I will comply, however, I will not respond to verbal calls. Barely, but I made it through yet another storm.

I have a hunch that Matt may have some these traits. Look up Borderline Personality Disorder. Therefore, be fair-warned that you will lose if you play with his ego. It's too powerful a force to go up against. I know you've tried for years, so don't think this is the time you will be victorious. I plan to starve my ex-wife of conflict by giving her nothing back. She hits the ball in my court; I turn my head and walk away. Eventually, I know, she will tire and find someone else to play with. Trust me when I say that walking away is best. Besides, with these gas prices, walking is a more sustainable and thrifty thing to do, right? Damn. A tank of gas shouldn't cost more than the car it's going in!

Leah De Luca   4/13, 8:46pm

Crazy day at work with possible layoffs. You have no idea! There are tiger teams in place preparing "contingency plans" for the possible layoff. Employees are fearful of what might happen – these are tough times. Fear truly inspires unsavory behaviors in people and fear within divorce proceedings is no exception.

I was going back to some of what you wrote about reflecting on your past with the football team. Isn't it surprising so many years later that hurtful past experiences tend to stick with us? It's a challenge to try to deflect those experiences from influencing our perspective as it is today. Yet, HOW we choose to let it influence us certainly is possible to determine.

When I was pursuing my graduate degree, I remember writing a paper that used "memetics" as a theory for human perception. Not sure if you're familiar with it. "Memes" from "memetics" is akin to genes from genetics, but instead of the physical DNA, the memes are the DNA of the mind. Memes are "mind viruses," or as quoted from an Internet article, they are "contagious ideas, all competing for a share of our mind in a kind of Darwinian selection." As memes evolve, they become better and better at distracting and diverting us from whatever we'd really like to be doing with our lives. They are a kind of drug of the mind. I often ask myself, how much of my current perception has evolved from the memes or mind viruses that came from my life's experiences with Matt or negative childhood experiences that I've carried into adulthood? Memes have a way of replicating and spreading, like a virus, and I think this is why we sometimes lose our foundation and slip backwards. On a daily basis, we make conscious decisions to confront those ideas when they surface, and challenge them to force a new way of thinking. For most people, it is natural to perceive through the old lens, yet for others, it's an awareness and a conscious choice to think and behave in a different way. While it may feel unnatural sometimes, at least in those moments when we want to float back, over time it becomes more natural; the old memes are destroyed by new ones.

I think about Matt, and in your case, your ex-wife or mom, and their memes and about how it makes them tick. I ask myself, what is it for Matt, past or present, that causes him to perceive the world as he does? I don't have the answers, clearly, but thinking about it helps me gain my own new perspective. The more days that pass, the more I feel peace about what is happening in my life. The more I come to accept it and the more I let go. Perhaps the old saying that "time heals all wounds" really is true.

That's not to say there still aren't really tough days. There are. But actually, the hard days are turning into hard moments. I think I'll always have some part of me that will yearn for what could have been, just as I did for 30 years of yearning for what could be.

I'll be heading back to Delaware in a couple of weeks, as my gig in NY is coming to an end. I'm so glad I did it. It was great on every possible level. Here, I believe the "Big G" intervened on my behalf. I am grateful.

Craig Shoemaker 4/13, 10:19pm

This weekend's comedy special shoot was one of my all-time best moments. It was like the culmination of all the hard work and hard knocks I put into a 30-year career, all paid off in one hour-and-a-half long special. I trained for this as if I was a world-class athlete, honing my skills leading up to the big event. I studied; I tried different performing techniques, and worked out. Now, I'm fit and weigh less than I have in 15 years. With my mind clear and spirit tended, I took that stage and owned it.

I gave them me, all of me. Nothing hidden – honest and committed material, based on my life as it is today. I enjoyed myself and the confidence grew with each joke told, commanding the stage. I actually greeted the audience as they walked into the theatre, choosing to connect with the crowd and welcome them to my party. I also came out during the opening warm-up act, to ad lib and give an indication of the fun we were going to have. Funny, my prep was different than at any other time in my career. Before, I accomplished things using sheer determination and strength whereas this time, I co-created with a higher power. The guy I tour with told me afterwards, "Bro, it was a 'ten.' I knew you were on it when you asked us to leave your dressing room so you could meditate." He was right.

I was guided by purpose, not my ego. Self-importance was replaced by service. I made it about the laughter, rather than what I would get out of it. The day of the shoot, I posted on Facebook how grateful I was to all who were a part of this journey, and asked that they give their memories of my show from the last three decades. Leah, I was filled with overwhelming emotion when I read what people wrote on my wall. They expressed the most beautiful sentiments and thanked me for giving them pleasure through the years. Some even pointed out specific moments when they remembered laughing the most they had in their lives.

The thought that I had created those great recollections for them hit me as never before.

I drove to the venue by myself; a two-hour drive in Friday L.A. traffic. On the way, I decided to call some of my purposeful peeps. I got a hold of Dave Cerami and cried with him, feeling so supported and understood. He kept telling me, "You deserve it buddy!" To be recognized for the work I have done feels amazing. Doing big shows in the past, I usually took the safe way. (I know this is hard to comprehend, since there is nothing "safe" about standing in front of people for 90 minutes!) No easy route this time. I decided to walk on and begin anew, to let the audience know exactly who I am. The emcee announced my name. I walked without the lifelong, uncomfortable, insecure piston-like bounce in my stride. I took the stage in quiet confidence and fluidly went to the middle with a large grin on my face. The audience, whom I had just spoken to minutes before, was cheering with great passion…they were family.

What a perfect evening. The crew, producers, agents and managers all looked me in the eye and affirmed that it was a major hit; the best they had ever seen. I celebrated with a big meal afterwards with a few comrades and my agent, knowing with confidence that this was a game changer. However, I drove home in solitude, wishing I that could share my joy with my family of origin. My mother and sister obviously struggle with similar issues as my ex-wife, holding only self-interest, and no care about what I might be doing to be happy. It's odd that here I am on top of the world, and yet, I'm still trying so hard to make my mom and sister notice and love me. That night I had 900 people yelling for more of me while the ones I love want nothing to do with me. It is so difficult. I can't even talk about it any more as the pain sears my skin like muriatic acid...

Leah De Luca   4/14, 6:48am

Wishing we weren't on completely opposite schedules, I wake to read this amazing entry and could never do it justice in the 1/2 hour I have before going to work. Words can't describe the feelings I had when I read about the show and every deliberate and natural step you took, to bring you to a place of such purity and service. Congratulations Craig, from my heart.

Leah De Luca 4/14, 7:53pm

Can I ask you a question? Do you love your mom? If so, what, specifically, do you love about her? If you don't love her, that's ok too. I just really want to learn about what you feel about her and why. I know how you feel about what she says and does but I'm not sure what you feel about "her." I get that you can't really separate it all, but still. You've spoken of just wanting to be acknowledged for the man you are. Let's just say she's simply not capable of this, for whatever reason. My question for you is, what's left for you?

I go back to something you told me a long time ago and that was to let go and let God. This is serious stuff. Letting go is so empowering. You taught me that! You've often spoken of surrendering to yourself and to higher power. That's what's in order here. Yet, something draws you back. Why? As much as being shut out by Matt has been hurtful, sometimes I wonder whether it's for the best. The reality is we struggle to co-exist on the level that I yearned and yearn for. That doesn't mean I still don't have feelings for him. Could it be the same for you and your mom? Acceptance may be the healing order of the day.

As for me, lately it feels so unnatural to pretend that Matt isn't in the picture. One of my shortcomings is that I can become pretty emotional. I cry easily. I actually despise this about myself though, both Matt and the kids used to tease me lovingly when I would cry at stupid commercials or when watching any movie of substance. I know for a fact, that seeing me tear up or cry about serious things in our own lives, makes my kids uncomfortable. I'm to the point now where I apologize in advance before having a tough conversation with them because inevitably, I'll shed a few tears. I don't do this to manipulate, to create guilt, to get sympathy, or for any other reason. I'm just freaking emotional. Period. Always have been. Pisses me off.

At any rate, I am looking forward to opening up this door and talking with my kids. I'm thinking I'll talk with them all together. To be honest, I'd love it if they'd be open to seeing a therapist and I plan to suggest that too. Not all of my kids are as far along on their spiritual journey and I'm thinking it'll be tough sell. I am proud to say that I have apologized to them on occasions where I know I've not been the best example, or when I've let them down. Funny, they want to let me off the hook when I do that and I won't let them do it! But as you said, "It's when you show that human side to your children that they are free." I hope that my kids see me as a strong woman but also as someone who is human, vulnerable, and makes mistakes but learns from them and remains on a path of love and compassion.

At any rate, I find it pretty interesting that you've reached this place in your career and have such fulfillment in who you are. You have this same fulfillment in your home with your wife and kids. You have this as well, with Dave Cerami; a better brother than any of the biological kind, and you are surrounded by the love of many friends and perfect strangers.

 Craig Shoemaker   4/14, 9:04pm

Do I love my mom? The answer is yes. I love her uniqueness and sense of humor. Laura is quirky; something that can also get in the way, but the eccentricities generally make me smile. We have had some great laughs with one another. I cannot begin to count the incredible memories she and I share, and Laura is much of the guy I am today. And I love me some Jersey Shore! (Not those greasy idiots on the TV show!) To this day, I schlep my entire family cross-country to vacation there.

My take is that now that I'm an adult, our relationship is quite different than when I idolized her as a child. There was a time when I thought she knew everything, as if she was a living Google. I went to her for answers when I was confused. She seemed so smart and gifted me with one important commodity – she influenced me to be worldly. It was important to her that I find my way around. I recall her telling me how to take the train to Center City and figure out for myself how to maneuver through the bustling metropolis of Philadelphia. We went to countless movies together, rarely avoiding anything typically considered inappropriate to a kid. I learned early on how to be a survivor too, often left alone to figure out how to manage obstacles. I still carry that poise today.

That said, there is a yin to the yang of my mom. She made me independent as a way to basically get rid of me. I was a burden for her. The biggest problem with her is her overriding self-obsession. At times, it is unbearable to be around. She shows zero interest in anything that does not fit her standards, often dictating and controlling to the point of emotional bullying. I told you how much I love the shore; well, my mom invites my sister to join her for a summer week, because Lizzy submits to the control by living blocks from Mom, but does not even ask my wife and kids to join her on her vacations, while always asking Lizzy to come down. If I say something, I am labeled a complainer or jealous. Can't have alternative feelings or express them in their world.

Do I accept her for the way she is and just deal with the crumbs and make them into cake? I gotta say, it hurts so much to be on the other side of her meanness. I think she hates men; and I am one of them. When I was a boy, I didn't notice it as much, but for many years now I am cognizant of her shutting me out. Her selfishness has also removed her from behaving in motherly ways. It's all about her and how she expects me to kowtow to her needs. She might give me a little nod or pat if I comply with her wishes. However, I long for so much more. I don't like the way I feel around my mother. She doesn't see me, hear me, or even truly love me. She has never said, "I love you." Tough to comprehend and even tougher to accept. This is why I go back for more, hoping that some day she will see the light that I am.

 Leah De Luca 4/15, 1:11am

I have to tell you, I enjoyed reading those words about what you love about your mom. It was so nice to hear you acknowledging that small part of her that you connected to. Makes her more real to me, in spite of not feeling I can relate to her on the "mom" level. I actually wondered whether some part of your talent and love for laughter come from her? In reading what you say about your perception that she hates men – that could well be true. Yet you continue to look for a void to be filled, small as it may be in the scheme of your life's blessings. You know what? That's okay with me. Something tells me that you may never be able to fully put the need for your mom's love totally aside. I think you should let yourself off the hook for that. Take each day as it comes. You never know when something new will be revealed to you...a new approach, a new perspective. Love is always worth trying for, so long as you don't let disappointment get the better of you. As the saying goes, "Never underestimate your ability to change yourself and never overestimate your ability to change someone else."

Leah De Luca   4/18, 5:32am

Came home from NY this weekend only to discover that Matt has begun taking things of value from the house; a painting, some high tech gadgets, etc. My attorney thinks I have the right to change the locks since Matt hasn't been living at the house and because he is not supposed to be helping himself to anything until things are settled. However, I fear wakening the sleeping giant again. If I listen to my lawyer's advice, I know Matt will see me as an evil person who locked him out, denying him access to "his" things. That said, if I do nothing, this will likely continue and I remain the perpetual doormat. Seems like a no-win situation. I'm less bothered by what Matt took than the fact that he did so without so much as the courtesy of letting me know or asking.

I'm actually feeling ready to clean house as I imagine that it will feel good to let go of some of the reminders of the past. I've basically decided that with the exception of the kid's bedrooms, there really isn't anything I want except things of sentimental value, photographs, special ornaments or gifts, etc. Things like our furniture, appliances, TVs, mean absolutely nothing to me.

I keep thinking about what I want my life to be like going forward. I don't want to settle into the comfortable of what was my life before! Instead, I want to expand my thinking and my relationships. I want to surround myself with people who lift me up spiritually, emotionally. I want to stop spending time with people who use me, or drain me, or bring me down, and there are still a few people like that whom I allow into my world. I want to make something, maybe a quilt, and give it to someone I love. I want to be a better person and influence change. Good change. Maybe I want too many things. I don't know. But it feels good to put it out there. I'm anxious for this chapter in my life to be over. Craig, I think I am finally ready to break free from the past and experience the next phase of my journey in life.

Craig Shoemaker   4/18, 11:30pm

Interesting what you wrote about house cleaning. Reminds me of a story…I grew up in a home that put little importance on neatness and organization. We accumulated crap, value-less in every sense of the word. My father paid zero child support and my mother barely got by on the limited salary she made at the law firm, so we weren't exactly stocking up on valuable family heirlooms.

About nine years ago, my mom boxed up some goodies from my old room and sent them to me with a note saying that they were encumbering the space she was making for her new husband in my old room. After laughing at the contents of the box, I wrote a one-man show about the contents of the 18x24x12 container that represented my life from ages 5-20. The performance ends when I finally reveal my childhood "valuables" to the audience, an odd assortment of worthless junk.

First, a penny collection, a seemingly innocuous item, but it actually says a lot about my early years. It was the one and only thing of mine that held any "value" whatsoever: three booklets of pennies in their respective holes, dating all the way back to 1909. Incidentally, I tried to cash them in a few months ago, hoping for a big payday. Turns out the whole collection was worth...well..."pennies." The next goodie was a plastic ruler, which had black and white pictures of the 1972 Phillies on it. Some player photos were blacked out, since I took a pencil eraser and removed them if they were married. If they were not eligible to marry my mother, they got erased!

Then, two homemade bamboo pot pipes, carved and made into bowls for smoking reefer. I remember selling these whittled crafts to a few kids even un-cooler than me. I also went into the fake ID biz in high school and a few of these creations were also contained in the box. I had my uncle steal U.S. Navy credentials so I could fill in the names and ranks with my Remington typewriter. My whole gang of teen buddies were "Seaman E-3s," which meant we we'd been enlisted for three years, even though we had long *Boogie Nights* hair and looked 12. Those homemade ID cards wouldn't look authentic to Stevie Wonder, let alone a bartender!

The trophies I found in the mystery container were plastic and basic, year-end participation rewards, except for a number of them from a camp where I dominated on Olympic Day against other local camps. These trophies represented one of the few victorious and empowering days from my youth, where I set records for speed and other athletic prowess. Truth be told, I cheated my age by 6 months to put me in the 12 & under category. Since I had not yet hit puberty, I figured that to be ok. I had lousy, torn-up sneakers, so I ran all events in bare feet. To this day I feel like no one can beat me sans shoes; like a Kenyan in a marathon.

Speaking of athletics, I also found a pillowcase from a cheer-leader, Luanne Phillips, who must have drawn the small straw when she got me as her "pep" assignment for Spartan football players. She painted my name and "Go Spartans!" with all sorts of inspirational encouragement. My mom also sent my Varsity jacket from that same football season. I recall dreaming of driving a cool car with a sophomore hottie, proudly wearing my cool Springfield Undefeated Football jacket, while she put a hickey on my muscular neck. But none of that ever happened. Instead, my drunken uncle took it and used my coat for a blanket when he was homeless, his vomit stains and all still located on the big, varsity "S." Good to know it had years of good use.

The mystery box my mom sent had trinkets, ticket stubs and old programs, some with autographs of pro baseball players I had stalked in stadium parking lots. One program was from the four days I'd like to forget – the time I was kidnapped and molested. That weekend in Washington DC was a turning point for me, being the pivotal moment in my life when I realized that I had to fend for myself in the world, becoming totally self-reliant. I was 13 years old, but I shot to an adult 30 that weekend. Now I have a keepsake reminder of it all, making it to the Eagles/Redskins game and back and living to tell the story.

The most telling relic my mom sent me was a birthday card. Actually, I saved lots of them, some from people who have been dead for 30 years, but there was one that stood out above all others. It said, "To the best son a father could have!" It was signed, "Love, Dad." When I discovered this among all the other cards, it made me recall its origin. I was 6 years old and knew at that time my father was certainly not going to express love to his only son. So, being the smart, enthusiastic and dream-filled person that I still am today, I devised a way to get what I wanted.

I took my lemonade stand money and bought the birthday card for myself. I went to the local drug store and plunked down 35 cents for a card from the "relative birthday" Hallmark section, then forged my father's name after the printed sentiment, with the "Love" being overly pronounced and large

CRAIG SHOEMAKER

before the "Dad" signature. I have to admit, when I found this card, I roared with laughter. I couldn't stop, even giggling at the way I wrote "love" with a backwards "e," Funny, I wanted something I couldn't even spell, much less receive.

CHAPTER EIGHT

ACCOUNTABILITY

Leah De Luca

Hey there. Been a busy week for me getting back to Delaware. In some ways glad to be back, yet in others, I feel like I'm thrown back in this insane process of divorce! I know I've said it a thousand times but divorce SUCKS! Matt is still not communicating with me. He knows it hurts me, and it's all he has left. My efforts to have a civil discourse to seek healing and forgiveness have gone unanswered. I feel like a moth batting myself against the light bulb outside, being attracted to something that only ends up hurting me when I go after it.

Tough week. I finally moved all of Matt's clothes into the spare room. Felt good to do some of that house cleaning we talked about, however, I cried as I took each of the familiar shirts off of the hangar, the same shirts I remember hugging with Matt in them. I thought of places we were together when he wore certain things and cried, which in turn, made me cry more. Yet I just kept going, moving the clothes into different space outside of my own.

It's still so surreal, though. And such an emotional roller coaster. I still feel that this divorce is more right than wrong but I can't help but wonder, "What if I had tried one more time? What if I regret this?" Ultimately, with each hurt that Matt hurls my way, my brain tells me, "Leah, you're doing the right thing." But, it's my heart that struggles. I remember what was good and I want to block out all that wasn't. But if I am being honest, I have to admit there wasn't nearly enough of the "good" during our marriage to feed my soul. I mourn for what could have been and yet, I also celebrate what lies ahead for me. I celebrate who I am; my independence, my freedom, the ability to be "me" for the first time since I was 15 years old. I enjoy getting to be me, not having to be something to someone else.

Interestingly, I do a lot more observing of other couples and relationships these days. It's as if I want to analyze everything and everyone. Gets on my nerves…trying not to over-think or over-analyze things, so I need to stop. Now, I just want to experience life as it comes at me. Nothing more, nothing less.

Craig Shoemaker   4/28, 8:26pm

I can relate! Big time. Even the part about the latching on to the good parts. I did the same, looking at the positives I could find, even though they were few and far between. I'll tell you this, there is nothing today I find positive! Holy shit. I am in it again with her. She brings the loco and I bite that burrito. She has a ploy she uses that locks me into the old pattern. Not our old pattern, but MINE. I practically LOOK for a fight now, responding with venom and tenacity as if my life is threatened.

Okay, so I decided that it is time to give you the ultimate story of my largest moment of growth and change in this endurance-test of self. I may have mentioned it before but now is the time to describe it, with the intention of getting back to what is good for everyone.

To begin, we need to go way back to January, six years ago, when I was way deep in the divorce process. Nothing was working for me, or so it seemed. I began searching for answers everywhere. "Struggle" was written on my face, so all in one day, not one, not two but THREE different friends told me to check out the "Landmark Forum," a weekend self-help seminar. Ok, G, I can take a hint! So, I attended the three-day class with an attitude of giving it all I had. I dove in with vigor, pleasing an old friend and veteran of the Forum, Vanda. She commented during recess about how cool it was to see a man remove the binding ties and fully participate. I did the work they suggested and volunteered as much as I could without being obnoxious.

They say the way you treat this education is reflective of the way you are in life. How true! Started strong and enthusiastic but as time wore on, I got restless, wanting better and sooner results. So I began to stew and resent. Then I panicked, thinking that my intended agenda would not be met. Sunday rolled around and I began to feel really restless and irritable, however, I disguised those feeling as indifference. Vanda wasn't there anymore to keep me in check and I became more childlike. I felt it was my turn for the leader to deal with my "more important" case of how to handle an ex who accuses you of molesting children. Hours ticked by. The closer we came to the conclusion of the event, the more intense I felt in my desire for the facilitator to point to me. I wanted specific answers to my problems. I paid a load of money for this shit! I was mad at the guy for not dealing with my divorce quandary and now viewed the retreat as a complete waste of time and money. So, I walked out like a brat and shocked Mika when this newfound frustration walked through our front door. Before, I had been excited to tell her about my progress. What a turnaround…

I went back to work at the radio studio, dejected. Pissed off too! I was in my righteous mode where no person, place or thing could take me away from this space. Then, one of my friends who had recommended the retreat called to check in. I was a little short and basically told him the Forum didn't do for me what it had done for him, and I fired up my engines about my ex-wife, lawyer, etc. Then, Vanda phoned. She was stunned by my attitude. She and I went back and forth for a while. However, I remember one very important exchange, something like this:

"You know, Vanda, I am the type
who's always evaluating and
addressing my part in all I do.
I've worked on finding my role
in this conflict with my ex,
being accountable… even humble."

Vanda responds; "Craig, you're right. You don't
have a role in it. YOU are one
hundred percent responsible for
creating this mess, and only you
can clean it up. None of the
answers you seek come from your
ex. You made all this happen
and are not a victim at all. No one is."

Tough words to take. I thought about how I created my reality, about Vanda's sage words about victimization, and then about how I related to my ex-wife in a manner that would never move us forward to achieve what I wanted for our broken family. Then I got a call from my lawyer, admonishing me for writing another bad note to my ex, where I called her a whack job.

I then paused to realize that if I were inviting my ex-wife into a new realm of communication/possibility, why would she ever RSVP to my invitation addressed to "Dear Whack Job"?? And that's when the light went on. This was when I made a decision to try out a new way of "being."

So I wrote a letter to Debby, putting aside all resentment and anger, and simply took responsibility. Not ONE comment about her behavior. The words flowed out of me with great ease. Words, which minutes before were tainted with defense. I introduced a new and refreshing framework. I didn't tell her what she should or shouldn't do, didn't admonish her for her heinous acts of cruelty. Instead, I let a compassionate higher source take over the writing. As I moved my fingers on the keyboard, it became easier with every breath. Humility was much more accessible than I had thought! The more I wrote, the more I realized that I HAD created this mess!

I sent the note and then the phone rang. I picked it up; it was my ex-wife, speechless and tender. She said, "Thank you, Craig. This is the man I married." A palpable shift took place. More tomorrow…

Leah De Luca   4/29, 5:32pm

Your story continues to move and inspire me in all kinds of ways. To me, it doesn't matter when you screw up, because you are someone that I want to emulate. Tons of respect for who you are.

CHAPTER NINE

UPHILL BATTLES

Leah De Luca   5/3, 9:56pm

Matt called me. The first time I'd heard his voice in months. My heart dropped. We didn't talk long but he wanted to let me know that his cousin (someone he is very close with) is in the hospital in critical condition. It was so surreal. Here he was, talking with me, crying about what was happening and this was the first time I've spoken with him in months, after countless attempts to reach out with no result. My heart aches for Matt's family. Still, I couldn't help but think, *Why is he calling me? What does he want or expect me to do?* Such conflicting feelings.

I cried with him and told him how sorry I was that this was happening and that I would pray for him. I asked him if there was anything I could do, then I asked if he would keep me updated. That's pretty much it. He later sent me a text thanking me for being there for him and he wrote, "I'm sorry for everything else." THIS, is what stuck with me. "I'm. Sorry. For. Everything. Else." Wow! Does he mean it? Is this something fleeting in a moment of sadness and need? I guess I shouldn't over-analyze. Here I go wanting to make cake out of what are likely crumbs. The story of my past life with Matt. Still, I latch on to this "once-in-five-months" expression of humanity and forgiveness. Stopping mid-stream here...

Craig Shoemaker   5/3, 8:15pm

Don't stop!

Leah De Luca   5/4, 3:24am

I guess the best part about what happened was that in those short 10 minutes, our conversation had NOTHING to do with the divorce. Nothing to do with our agendas. Rather, it was two people, feeling shock and sadness, giving each other support. What a feeling of relief to have a conversation with Matt that wasn't filled with fear, anger, and resentment. We've continued to exchange a few text messages but only about his cousin's status. I guess I am hoping that amidst this tragic development that maybe, just maybe, a spark of compassion and forgiveness can be ignited within Matt. If it is, I'm here to blow air on it to build the bigger fire.

Leah De Luca   5/4, 7:03pm

Update: Matt's cousin took a turn for the worse a few hours
ago and Matt called to let me know. It is very tragic and makes
the divorce and any other problem I have seem insignificant.
Thanks for your prayers and support from afar. I appreciate it.

Leah De Luca   5/7, 4:23am

I really need to talk with you. Matt is very distraught. He
sent me a message asking about something I confided to
you. I think I know what happened here. I sometimes write
you outside of FB and then copy/paste in the private FB
message. I think Matt hacked into my computer and found
my private writings. One, in particular, was when I wrote you
about knowing that marrying Matt could be a mistake. I can't
believe he would invade my privacy. I am going to talk with
him, possibly meet with him later today. Here's where I need
your help. On one hand, it angers me that he took these
liberties and violated my privacy but then on the other, I think
about how it must have made him feel. So taking a step back
and trying to put myself in his shoes, I see that he is deeply
hurt. I feel so bad for causing that.

Craig Shoemaker   5/7, 1:45am

Been thinking about your situation. Look, I basically only
know you from our exchanges, but you have so much emotional, creative and intellectual depth at your fingertips. It
is right here in the history of your letters. As I read them,
it becomes more and more evident that the more you peel
away the layers of the onion, the more whole you become.
And you cry a lot, so the onion analogy is perfect for you! In
all seriousness though, if you re-read what you wrote over
the past several months, you would see your zest blossom.
You have lived many years within the unhappiness of not
serving your own spirit.

Actually, I think this recent crossroads is an opportunity. I
was going to say "opportunity in disguise," but it is not hidden
at all because it has been in your face for decades. Only
now, you are willing to say, "Enough!" As far as I understand,
you claim to be done with this old paradigm and through
this, have begun to unlock freedom. I don't mean the literal
freedom from being divorced but the liberation of your own

soul. Too many times have you swayed away from expression of true self, only to become a tiny version of it because you were convinced that you are not enough as-is. You were taught to carry out your life in certain ways, ways that served others, but not YOU.

I encourage you to remain committed to self. Being committed to you is not selfish. You already know this, but when provoked, I can see that you lose trust in the process. This moment IS your moment. Carpe diem! Bathe in the light and turn away from your temptation to return darkness. Be you, the bright and shining person you are destined to be.

Leah De Luca   5/7, 4:38am

Thank you so much for writing this, even after being up all night, you inspire me in ways most others can't. I plan to re-read what you wrote a few times today before I talk with Matt. I feel like I just got the pep talk of my life!

Craig Shoemaker   5/7, 1:45am

One more thing. I suggest that you do not meet with Matt in the near future. No good can come out of it, especially when you are this vulnerable.

Leah De Luca   5/11, 6:53pm

Hey there, how are you? A bit calmer here, at least for the moment. Sadly, Matt's cousin passed. Matt and I haven't spoken about the issue that arose concerning my communication with you since I told him I would not meet to discuss it. Yet, he has managed to be able to continue to communicate with me concerning the status of his cousin throughout the weekend, and even let me know about the funeral arrangements.

I'm a little anxious about going to the funeral but in my heart, I want to be there, even though it'll be rough seeing all of his family for the first time in months. Maybe out of tragedy, there will be an opportunity for healing. I feel like I've diverted our conversation to just what is happening with me, which is kind of trivial given recent events. By the way, since I believe that the "Big G" brought you to me on this journey, I now have you saved in my cell phone as "Big G". Reminds me of how you became a friend.

Craig Shoemaker 5/16, 10:44pm

I am so sorry to hear about Matt's cousin. You are going through such change already that this passing must be so difficult for you and your family right now. Deepest condolences.

I'm home now, and it feels good. After being away, the hugs and kisses are even more delicious & breathtaking. Johnny especially seems to be bringing his unique expression of love in an even bigger way. Last night, he literally leapt into my arms, holding me with such conviction. I feel so gifted to have him, as well as the rest of the "Shoe Crew." It makes me reflect on how happy I am that I fought to retain my parental rights as a father.

I am also glad to hear you speak of your commitment to self. When things got really bleak, you stood firm in your willingness to find and develop your own story, not Matt's. You were so brave to remain solid in this foundation that you are forming. Sure, it may have felt like the concrete is moist and murky, but how good did you feel when you said "no" to the request to go back to being told how to think and feel? So proud of you!

Leah De Luca 5/17, 8:17pm

So it started with the viewing on Friday night. Had to muster up all the courage I had to be there. I arrived early to get in line. Within a few minutes, Matt's sister Olivia found me, greeting me with the warmest embrace. Of course we both cried and hugged, expressing how much we missed each other and how sad the reason was that we were there. This was similarly repeated with each and every encounter with Matt's family that night.

I finally made it up to the casket, not far from where Matt was standing. Wasn't sure how to approach him so I extended my hand and gave him a warm and genuine hug. It was a hug that is hard to explain as it expressed my condolences and sadness for what the family was going through, and yet at the same time, it was a hug to express forgiveness and a will to move forward. Matt was gracious and kind, thanking me for being there.

At the funeral the next morning, I watched as Matt walked in by himself, with the kids behind him. This tore me up inside. I felt all kinds of emotions. I felt turmoil inside because I was missing Matt and his family. I wanted to jump up and be there with them rather than watching from afar. Emotion flooded me as I felt a sense of loss for Matt's cousin, and a sense of loss for me and my kids, our family...Matt. I wavered in between crying for the loss of a wonderful person, and the loss of a marriage at the same time. Went through lots of tissues but ironically, it felt really good.

I'm happy that my kids are home this weekend. I need their warm spirits in the home. Brings me such joy and peace, it's inexplicable. Their presence this summer couldn't come at a better time with what lies ahead for me. Bottom line is, I feel good. I feel that each day is presenting opportunities to me to decide how I want to handle myself, to explore who I really am, and to express myself in ways that used to be suppressed, manipulated or controlled.

Craig Shoemaker   5/17, 8:59pm

Leah, I am blown away, lit up by seeing you go within for your answers. You're not giving up on your path to inner Shangri-La and I am so pleased to bear witness to such strength and conviction. This stuff ain't easy and it most certainly is not for the weak.

I had something happen today that made me think of you...

So I'm at this business symposium. A guy comes up to me with a hunch that maybe I could help him with certain business initiatives and so forth. Then, out of the blue, he tells me that his sons (ages 8 and 10) had been kidnapped by their mom and taken to Chile. I took a deep breath and went in deeper. To tell you the truth, it was a similar breath I took when I wrote you back for the first time, checking in with higher source to guide me. I was very present and became fully available to this man. Then, two strangers in a large vestibule of a hotel in Hollywood broke down in one another's arms in tears. I embraced a man I had only met moments before and assured him that all was going to be all right in the end. Moreover, I pledged that I would stay with him in support.

I went inside for lunch while he wiped away his tears in the bathroom. My good friend Bob was there. I began to tell him what had gone down, when I lost it again! Then…I got it.

When we feel the power of the highest sense, the presence of light within knocks us sideways. When divine current flows unimpeded, there is a shockwave! In those moments, our tears are being moved by something we have no control over. Our self-will and fears are removed in the moments when weeping begins. What I felt today was a palpable connection to the divine source. I was led to meet this man in conscious energy and our bond was pure and sound. When we have these vulnerable pauses amid our speedy process, it is a reminder of how beautiful life is when we slow down and allow for nature to take over and identify a force of pure love. So, next time you think you are being a baby when you cry, just know that babies are more connected to G than adults are. Unadulterated and unfettered by mankind, an infant is God incarnate. How incredible.

 Leah De Luca   5/25, 5:01am

Not even sure where to begin, but the past couple of weeks have been filled with every kind of emotion. I have met with Matt twice since the funeral. In hindsight, not sure I was totally ready for it. I so desperately want some kind of healing for us and I always think communication is key to that process. I want to be able to work through this process and our pain but I think I have been more optimistic and anxious to talk with him than I was probably ready for.

A few things that came out of these meetings: He expressed not knowing "…how it all has come down to this." He expressed sorrow and his intention to begin stepping up to "help" more. We talked at length about our families and how each of us has been holding up. I did fall apart at one point, letting Matt know how hard things have been on me. He apologized for that and again said he intends to "help." We both talked about what we were going through and the things we missed about being together. We laughed…and we cried. At that point things seemed to be going well.

Then we had a second meeting as a family, with our kids. It was awkward for them to have us altogether and it was strange for Matt and me, too. We had agreed to do this to show the kids we could be united when it came to issues concerning them. After dinner, the kids left and things went downhill from there. Matt needed to get a lot off of his chest. There was lots of anger and lots of questioning. I found myself right back in that place that I was in during my marriage; feeling emotionally abused, threatened, wrongly accused, misunderstood, disrespected. It was like a flashback of epic proportions. Still, Matt professed his love for me. I told him that I still care deeply for him…but that it wasn't enough. It felt like pure insanity. One minute, he's directing hatred towards me, and the next he's declaring genuine love.

In the end, we talked about the possibility of making the divorce process less formal. I suggested we skip depositions and try to come to agreement on some things without the lawyers. Yet I'm not holding out hope, as I am fairly certain he will not be willing to work out a fair settlement without his legal team. No matter, I had to try. I find myself wondering today – did I do the right thing in meeting with him? It was like disturbing a hornets' nest. Not just for Matt, but for me, too. Things are still so raw. I vacillate between feeling for Matt, loving him in a way that I can't fully describe…and then to feeling ecstatic that I am close to being freed from a suffocating relationship.

 Craig Shoemaker   5/26, 9:01am

Now is the time of your greatest vulnerability. This is the time of reckoning for you, the moment where you choose the road to travel. The old, familiar path is so effortless; it's like breathing, as we know exactly what lies ahead because we are so trained in this form of engagement. We know this path and navigate it mindlessly. Yet it takes great conviction and courage to halt – to stop this dynamic, which has an illusion of success.

This is truly where the rubber hits the road, where great lives are found. As long as we no longer accept the human condition we have created for ourselves, we then can move into a brighter, lighter way of being. These are challenging times. Yet, I have deep confidence in you and me! Someday, we will be laughing on a mountaintop, taking in all the beauty, as the pain, suffering and sorrow are far in the distance, still there, but not a part of our presence. And I see you with the spiritual, good man of your dreams by your side.

Leah De Luca   5/29, 6:33am

Such a crazy few days. In my quest to seek a peaceful place of existence for Matt and me, I found myself on that familiar roller coaster ride. The good, the bad, and all that lies in between. Oh, the insanity of it all…

On Wednesday, I drove my daughter to Matt's sister's house so that she could pick up Matt's car to use it while hers was in the shop. Matt and I had agreed that I would drop her off after work that day. As I drove up to the house on the familiar street in the suburban neighborhood, a flood of emotions and memories filled me. So many amazing memories – always ones full of love and laughter. After I dropped off my daughter, I drove off very slowly as tears streamed down my cheeks. Somehow, in that moment, there was finality to it all.

When I got home, my niece was there to visit. It felt great to see her. I didn't look at my cell phone again for a couple of hours. When I did, I found a text from Matt reading, "Leah, why didn't you come in the house when you dropped Angie off? It was Mom's birthday." My initial thoughts included questions like, *Why would I go in? Do they expect me to go in and be a part of their lives even with all that has happened? Was it Matt who expected this? How did he arrive at this expectation? Did I do something wrong? Should I have known to go in?*

I responded by telling him I had not seen his text earlier and asking him to wish his mom a happy birthday. Then, I received this message, "Leah, this will be my last communication to you. I tried to make this work but you don't care about us." WTF? Where did this come from? My heart fell to the pit of my stomach. I thought, *Here we go again.* We make a tiny bit of headway in the past couple of weeks, and then I am left scratching my head wondering what I did or said to make him lash out and shut down. However, this time, I gave in to the idea that I will never be able to figure out what makes him tick…

Then, Saturday, Matt appeared at the house to take care of some things. He came and began chatting with me as if nothing had happened. My inner dialogue returned. *What the f is going on? Last night he hates me, this morning he's making pleasant small talk.* I asked him what gives with the text message and he "clarified" that he only meant he would...no longer talk about the divorce with me but that he intended to talk with me about other things. Flashback to the marriage: from anger, to love, to confusion, to lack of accountability, etc. During our marriage, one day would be very good while the next would be horrible. I found my anxiety level building over the weekend as I felt pulled back into the dark days of my past when Matt's power consumed me. As always, I coached myself back to center as I did so frequently during our marriage...this time, however, for the very last time.

Craig Shoemaker   5/29, 8:03pm

All too familiar, I'm afraid...Yet, I've learned that I make the decisions to create the life I want, not my ex. The rules of engagement are no longer in her hands, but soul-ly mine. Ego, either mine or someone else's, cannot run the show, for the results will be senseless and absurd, based on fear and illogical thoughts and emotions. Imagine if society existed upon standards dictated by whims and selfish desires. You would have anarchy and chaos. Nothing would be accomplished. Commitments broken. Love fleeting...

I think you and I made the initial mistake of putting faith into our exes. Each and every time we participate in their way of doing things, it compromises the system, like pouring sugar into a gas tank. People of this disorder know NO better. Their instinct, based on years of developing a system of being a victim and blaming others for all that goes down, is something they will never even pause with, just as a caged cat would do if you put your hand in there. Lions aren't thinking about consequences or accountability. No, it is all they know, to use their limited, but sharpened skills to take you out, and just go on eating without thought that their prey has a family and feelings.

I spent the Memorial holiday weekend immersing myself with family, participating in various activities, but not wandering far from home. Yesterday, we were invited to our friends, Mikki and Nadia's baby blessing and then on a men's hike. I have mentioned Mikki before, but to remind you, he is an extraordinary man, a cut above most.

Our family arrived at the Elevate Studios Campus in the beautiful and mountainous Ojai, California at 11am, as instructed by our invite. We had no clue what was in store, but with Mikki, we can always count on something extraordinary. Suddenly, IT became clear to me, a profound realization: "If we choose to hang with people of integrity and sound character, great events will come to pass." The opposite is certainly true too. Hang with crazy, and you will end up in a loony bin. My nut house is my own mind. The silent fighting in there, as I play many parts as if it was real dialogue, is more destructive than if I actually got punched in the eye. In my head, I am coming up with the right words to make Debby stop coming after me but in reality, it's a different, sad story.

The men all gathered around Mikki for our next three hours, my two oldest sons, Michael and Johnny, included. Mikki asked us to set a clear and focused intention for our day. I had not met anyone else in the group before. It was comprised of men of all different ages and ethnic backgrounds. The basic plan was this: we were to meditate, set strong intentions, walk in silence half the way, honor the land and infuse healing energy with each step. Along the way, we stopped to check in with one another to share our deepest thoughts. This was when I was struck with a second realization: *If we are with those who live significant and service-filled lives, the moments together will be rich and fulfilling.*

Mikki spoke humbly about what he has been through; starting with his relationship with his father, admitting there was still some residual effect from his dad's abandonment when he was a little boy. His admission made us all so much more comfortable, allowing for a clearer passageway for breakthroughs. There were a few fathers in the group, they tended to speak more than the single cats, but even in silence, much was being said. Leah, the radiance of special meaning that day was present and self-evident.

I talked about a number of things with the group when we stopped during the hike. My eyes filled up every time I opened my mouth. I couldn't help it! With every step, both literally and metaphorically, I felt more connected to my family, especially my sons, frequently rubbing Michael's head or gently patting Johnny on the shoulder. I kept thinking of how they were receiving this great gift, and how it would be remembered for a lifetime.

The good news is that both sons loved it too! Even though they didn't know Mikki well, both boys gravitated to him. Mikki treated them as fellow men, being "let in" on what it is like

CRAIG SHOEMAKER

when true and honest men gather to honor others and themselves. During the trek, he also asked us to pray and infuse goddesses into all that is around us, including our mothers. As you probably guessed, this was tough for me. However, I got a hold of a guy I respect and talked with him about her. This was when I thought of you. See, when I walked alongside these incredible dudes, I remembered how difficult it is for you to believe men of profound goodness exist. But, I'm here to tell you that they DO. I was walking with them!

Leah, you deserve to fly in that rarified air. I believe you can and will have this. Move in the direction of greatness. If you are to find a diamond in the rough, then you must search in places where you don't usually tread. I want you to have what you deserve. I know deep inside that you must release Matt to the universe. If he stays stuck in the system you two have built, how can he ever find his true self or potential? Conversely, if you stay entrenched in the current paradigm, how can you find yours? You two keep giving each other a safety net; so then how can you expect to learn to fly?

What I took in on this special weekend was that there were a bunch of men, who were like Matt and me at one time, all mired in the muck and having no clue how to get out. All of us have endured our own form of abuse/abusing others. But now, having righted ourselves, there are those of us who now walk in the shine. Awakened, but not until we liberated ourselves from our former spouses.

Leah De Luca   5/31, 8:08pm

Amazing stuff. So inspiring. I asked myself, "What moved me so much in reading your words?" And then I knew. They cut RIGHT to the core. Yes, it is SO very difficult for me to grasp that there are people of profound goodness out there. You have already shown me that it does, in fact, exist, but I still look at you as a very rare spirit in a sea of many who still buy into the old paradigms. You give me hope. Mostly, I have to thank you for also affirming that this is something I deserve and, hopefully, will someday have. I need to affirm this for myself so that I may begin my own journey toward a more spiritually fulfilling life. As I surround myself with those who are seeking to be on that same path, I realize that I am already on my way.

Yet it is so very easy to be lulled into the old way of thinking and behaving. Today, I am committing that I am going to take some real steps to break through the old patterns! I must and will develop my own plan and take the steps necessary to continue along this journey. Once again, I thank you. Your amazing weekend has re-charged me for the coming weeks and set my wheels into motion. Peace.

 Craig Shoemaker   5/31, 11:11pm

So gratifying to read. I am beyond happy to hear you commit to taking steps that you now know are worthy of attention. This has been my greatest key to living in the "home" I am in now. First, there must be an admission that old ways of behaving will never elicit desirable changes. Next, the words, "real steps" indicate that a person is ready to walk the walk. How wonderful for me to read this.

CHAPTER TEN

WINDS OF CHANGE

Leah De Luca   7/1, 4:56pm

So it has been a very strange couple of months, going all the way back to when Matt's cousin passed away. As you know, Matt began communicating with me then. In the past weeks, it's been the usual roller coaster with him. My emotions have been all over the map. The idea of being able to communicate with him after all those months was very appealing to me, though, I'll save you the suspense…he's no longer talking with me now. I'm back to sending messages through the lawyer for even the most mundane things.

Anyway, we had a couple of dinners together, talked on the phone and texted on and off, saw one another when he'd be here taking care of errands, etc. Overall, things were relatively civil. Recently my kids helped him move some furniture and the rest of his personal things to his place. Wow! That was hard to watch. I had to be there so we could agree on the stuff he was taking but watching him empty the house of his personal things made me have this sinking feeling in my gut. We both cried that day. He kept telling me that the divorce felt wrong and asking me if I was sure about it. And the reality was, Craig, I wasn't sure. I don't know if you had doubts when you went through all this. Now that you have your wonderful life with Mika, I'm sure you can easily say you are sure you did the right thing. I guess I'm not there yet. I want to be there but I definitely have some doubts – not enough to make me turn back, though.

What I realize is that Matt's communications with me were so appealing that I kept them going as long as I could. Maybe that was wrong of me. I realize that his somewhat improved behavior was completely about his desire to reconcile. He made this more and more clear over the course of several weeks. In between, there were tears, frustration, sometimes anger, even laughter. I was lulled into that familiar sense of hoping and wishing that I could have Matt the way I wanted him. The exact same feelings I had during the marriage.

Then something would go wrong again, and I'd waver between wanting to get the hell out and wishing desperately for a normal life with him. I wanted him, but I wanted him MY way. I wanted that unattainable "idea" of him. I wanted the Matt that made me really happy SOME of the time. I still want that in some ways. I recognize this familiar pattern of my life, latching on to those proverbial crumbs and stretching them as far as I possibly could. Over the past many weeks, I found myself allowing my feelings to take me wherever they wanted to, and then whack! My brain would inevitably give me the wake up call. My heart felt pulled into wanting to go back, yet, my head knows better.

I am so frustrated with myself, Craig. I feel like I haven't been able to fully let go as I should. The false hope that Matt can be the person that I want him to be is driving me nuts! I have to let go of the desire to have a friendship with Matt. He is simply not capable of it. Or maybe he is, but he knows I want this so badly that he uses this to manipulate me.

I guess the good news is that the "monster" that Matt became in my mind during these proceedings seemed to fade a bit as I saw the good in Matt again, even if only temporarily. He seems more human to me, instead of the silent adversary. That can't be a bad thing. Anyway, I have been spending my time with the people I love dearly. Been meditating too, in my quest to seek new experiences. I yearn for the day that my heart is truly open to new relationships. Still not there yet. One day....

Oh, I meant to tell you about a bit of irony! As I was emptying out some bookshelves for Matt on Father's Day, I stumbled on a small book I had given him seven years ago on our anniversary, entitled, *If I Only Knew... Gentle Reminders to Help You Treasure the People in Your Life.* Inside the cover I had written him the following note:

*Matt, May we always remember
to treat one another and others
we love as if it were the last
time we might be with them*
~ Love, Leah

The book wasn't some best seller but paging through it while Matt was outside loading up the truck, a couple of excerpts struck me. One read, "If I Only Knew... my choices, however small and seemingly insignificant were taking me away from you, I would turn around and run to you." Another, "If I Only Knew... that my past is no excuse for who I am now, that truth could have set me free to change." Next, "If I Only Knew... that it was wrong to put others under my own expectations and make them feel guilty, I would have stopped manipulating them and chosen love as the higher way." And finally, "If I Only Knew… that tomorrow was not coming, I would ask you to please forgive me for any wrong I may have done to you."

There are a couple of dozen other pages with similar messages in this small book. As I read it, of course while wiping away tears, I wondered to myself if he had ever read through it. Seven years later, the pages of the book were still crisp and new and the book was buried in a set of old encyclopedias on bookshelves in my basement. I vaguely recalled his reaction when I gave him the book years ago. Certainly not the kind of gift a macho guy like Matt would ever really appreciate. Maybe this was another attempt to express myself to him? What I wanted, how I wanted him to think and feel about me, about him, about the marriage? Who knows?

I contemplated giving him the book again that day, but I didn't. Instead, I kept it. I've since read through it a few times and while it stirs up emotions; it is nonetheless bringing me some peace and some strength. No matter what is going on in my life, it reminds me to stop and smell the roses, to appreciate all that I have and all that I am blessed with in my life. It makes me want to call my parents a little more often, hug my kids a little tighter, to tell my friends how much I appreciate them. So tonight I say to you, "I appreciate you, and all you've done to support me these last many months."

Craig Shoemaker   7/9, 6:57pm

Sorry, it has taken so long for me to get back to you. Been busy planning a surprise party for Mika's 40th birthday. She had NO clue what was waiting for her as we walked together to our neighborhood Community Center. I wanted it all to be perfect, as many people were attending to honor this incredible woman. I flew her mom in from Seattle. I was bracing for the bawl-fest when she laid eyes on her mom.

I was really stressed from, not planning a party, but that I had just heard that my sister and Debby had secretly made a rendezvous nearby. My sister flew 3000 miles from her home in Philly and only contacted my ex, the same ex who would have me jailed under false charges, instead of connecting with Michael and Johnny through Mika or me. They lied to Michael and Johnny too, putting them squarely in the middle, as the boys suddenly found themselves being sneaky, hanging out with my relatives, not their mom's.

Also, Lizzy and her kids have never met Jackson, which led to a stronger sting. It is so spiteful and hurtful and I processed some feelings with my wife as we headed to the party. As we were walking to the party, pushing Jackson in this stroller, I became acutely aware of the adoration I hold for my wife. I said to her, "I love you in a way that is indescribable because I never in my life experienced true love before. This is all new to me. Mika, is there any way I can demonstrate or express how much I love you? Can I make it bigger in any way?"

She said, "No, you can't. I love you every day, more and more each day. You show me by the way you look at me. You show me by talking to me in the way you are now. You show me by taking care of me, by giving me such an amazing life." Leah, the whole time I was thinking, *Well, you are about one minute from taking a show of love to a whole new level!* LOL.

She had never had a surprise party. I planned it like I had a CIA background. When it came time to walk over, Jackson was asleep, so I went into the shower, ran out quick and gave him a little shake to wake him. He let out a loud cry, and I yelled down, "Mika, I think Jackson is up!" Hey, he had to take one for the team! I knew for sure Mika had no idea what was about to go down. We walked into the Rec Center room. I dashed in front of her to get a better view. Wow! She lost her footing and her knees buckled, letting out such a sound. Then, the tears flowed as, one by one, family and friends came up to embrace her. Yes, love was there and it was gigantic. When people advise me to look at all I have, and ignore my ex, sister and mother, I didn't have to think on this one. Perfect timing. I welled up and smiled ear to ear, then caught Mika's eyes as she screamed with elation, "I love you so much!!" This is exactly what the doctor ordered. It was an affirmation that came not only from my wife and a room full of people, but from the divine...I am loved.

Leah De Luca　　　　　　　　　　7/10, 5:12am

Amazing! You two inspire me, honestly. The depth of your love for one another is so very beautiful. I know you appreciate every minute. It is obvious; you remember not to take one another for granted. This beauty negates any force of ill will or negativity your sister and Debby brought that day. Hope

the rest of your weekend is as wonderful as your evening last
night among loved ones.

 Craig Shoemaker   7/11, 6:13am

Okay. Here it is, the big enchilada I promised to write ages
ago, the largest of all the epiphanies in this divorce mess. As
I wrote a while back, I went to a self-development course and
eventually got to a place where I wrote a letter to my ex-wife
that took 100% responsibility in creating conflict. I began with
resistance but after writing each sentence, I made admis-
sions that were delivered aplenty with great ease. Once I
committed to myself that I would not poke, instigate or blame
her whatsoever, the self-promise turned into areas I had not
explored in the past.

I was steadfast in my goal of maintaining personal accountability. I spoke of the unreasonable expectations I put onto
her and others. I talked about how I invite conflict and don't
truly listen. I mentioned the needling I do and the difficulty
I have letting go. How I make people wrong if they don't
see my logic, instead of going further to see where they
are coming from. How I deem their perception to be off and
insane, which is actually crazy-making itself. All in all, the
self-revelatory note was one of my greatest works, and the
freedom I felt was enormous.

Another key component in that letter was admitting that I
have lied. The big lie I addressed was the one where I was
disingenuous with her. I spent all those years trying to do
what was right, instead of doing what was truth. The fact is,
she noticed when I was doing something to please her with
actions I thought she wanted, which in turn is very selfish.
You see, in going about the people-pleasing, I actually want
to look good, which in turn is really about me and not about
anything genuine. In the end, I came to the conclusion that
my behavior is not brimming with pathos as much as I'd like
to tell myself.

I lived a lie. As I said, I loved the idea and parts of my ex
but basically never truly loved my ex-wife, though I didn't tell
her that in the letter. I only mentioned that it's my inauthentic
actions that drove us to conflict and that she had nothing to
do with our troubles. As I wrote it, I realized how awful it must
have been for her to be married to someone who basically
used her to work through his mom shit! I wasn't seeing her

authentically; rather, I was using her as someone who would take on the role of a nurturing maternal influence; a role she could never fulfill or live up to. Through this, I realized that these unreasonable expectations set our marriage up for failure, therefore making it toxic.

I also lived a lie by promoting myself as a guy who does good things instead of being a man who IS all good things. When I am not involved in the "proving" business, I am actually a greater man than who I can ever profess to be. I was just thinking that I resent my ex for treating me with disdain. Ironically…or not, she hates most men because she has so many father wounds unresolved. Is my turning her into my mom any better than me being turned into her dad, Chuck? Here I am harping on my mother, sister and ex for them to see and hear me and yet, I turn others into what I choose to observe, not who they are at their core. I see and treat them as people who put too much stock into image and appearances. You can be sure they feel the same way about me!

I sent the amends letter and made sure to call her and ask her to open it, assuring her that it was a kind note of appreciation, not another of my rants that took her inventory (another thing I am accountable for). That's when she called back and cried with me and expressed sorrow, appreciation and a dash of love. Now, I'd like to say this lasted for years, or even a WEEK. I'd be lying if I did. But it did initiate the next step that was the big-time lift for all of us, leading me to where I am today; the man who sends these notes to you.

About a couple weeks after my ex received my "accountability" letter, we were scheduled to appear in court regarding a restraining order that I'd had the judge issue against my ex-wife and two of her brothers she had enlisted in this ugly game of hers. Before the proceedings, my lawyer had instructed me to not to say a word but I couldn't help myself. I am an emotional man, for better or worse, and hearing lies hurled against me was too much to endure.

Her rotund brother, red-faced and prepared to lie his ass off, takes the stand with that familiar attitude of righteousness I know all too well from living with his sis. The man lives 3000 miles away, is detached from his own family, much less knows anything about mine, and acts as if he's a former resident in my basement. I started reacting by rolling my eyes and turning my head in disgust when Susan, my old friend and family law attorney, promptly admonished me. She put a hand on my thigh to gently calm me down, knowing that her client's image was very important at this critical time. This was basically the judge's impression of me and it was not going well. Finally, as my ex-wife's brother said another lie about me, I let out a sound where I blew audible air from my lips. "Phht!"

Yikes. The judge did not take kindly to my gut reactions and he laid into me with venomous admonishment, threatening to throw me out of his court if I pulled that crap again. He postponed the proceeding until the following day.

I could not sleep that night. I was downtrodden to the point of wanting to give up. I was defenseless and voiceless, and it appeared I was going to lose all I had worked so hard to remedy. All the progress of repairing my name and getting equal custody looked to be out the window. I went to work the next day and shot a "Little Caesar's Pizza" commercial with a smile on my face, even though inside I was thoroughly distraught. Coincidentally, the commercial cast me as a dad with an angel on one shoulder and a mini-devil on the other, both giving me advice.

Something of Great Spirit suddenly took over. Instantly, I understood that doing things "the old way" would no longer serve anyone. As I was wrapping up the shoot, I began to feel a deep resolve. This reminded me of when Dorothy faces the Wicked Witch and is instructed to face her greatest fears; she looks up into the sky and sees the words, "Surrender Dorothy." Never before did this movie moment have so much meaning. I thought, *This is exactly what I need to do!* Surrender. Give up my fight to be right. Let go of my need to be understood. Throw away the self-serving desire to be viewed as perfect. Toss away the defects of character that have led to this horrific experience I was having in court and out. Take contrary action from one who wants to win, and replace it with actions of peace. Then let Big G handle this.

I jumped into my car and raced to get to the 12:30 pm court appointment with the angry judge. I was already feeling a freedom as I called my lawyer on the cell. "Susan, I decided to give up. I am not going to pursue restraining orders. All I ask is that we stand for Michael and Johnny and design a new standard of relating. What I'd like to do is issue mutual apologies to the court and state our intentions to focus on our children's welfare."

My attorney was livid. "I can't believe you are doing this, Craig. After all the work I have done and you are throwing it all away? The courts don't work this way. You see the world through rose-colored glasses." I let her know she had no clue as to what it is like to live like this and that this was my final decision. Fighting will only leave more scars. The peace begins with me. In the end, she conceded, saying she would run it by the opposing counsel. When I arrived at court, Susan informed me that my ex-wife and brother agreed to the terms. She grabbed the pages of my hand-written apologies. Turning to me, she said, "Craig, you know I love you but this is against my advice. I will read this to the court but I am done with this case after today. I just can't work like this."

That day, I had such grace and confidence, something I had not felt in a very long time. I simply let go and stepped into the courtroom, knowing everything would be okay, despite the stern warning from my attorney. Judge Stevens closed the chambers to all others. He began with a speech telling us he endorsed this new method of resolve. Susan nervously picked up the pile and began to read. Every word she said nudged more of a cleansing inside of me. It was palpable. An indescribable ball of clean energy replacing all the toxic buildup from years of battle! The waters were parting as she turned each piece of notebook paper. Then, I heard a stammer in her voice. I looked up, and her throat was throbbing. She paused, and then put her hand gently on her heart as she recited another admission from this man who had finally found his vision.

I felt the healing taking place right then and there. Susan tried to keep her professional composure, as a teardrop fell on to the fresh ink. She shook and cleared her throat, often stopping when something hit her soul. Nothing was going to stop this restoration! She read more of what I mentioned to you before – little Craigy becoming a man by having the maturity to admit my wrongs. I wrote about all the times I said terrible things to Debby, whether to her or behind her back, and made no excuse for it or "reason" why I did. I went into detail as to how I am passive-aggressive, often asking of Debby what I won't do myself.

Leah, gossip is an underrated killer, so I spoke of how I had done this, then committed to ceasing on the spot. I talked about the effects of my retaliatory actions, never mentioning that they were caused by her actions. Also stated in the apology letter was how many times I went off the course I so often claimed I was on. Gave the people listening a big ole buffet of self-reflection and a promise to change the self-righteous behavior, all the while never mentioning anything disparaging about Debby. There is an old "trick" folks use to remain non-accountable while appearing to be looking at self – to make "apologies" in a manner that is a reaction, instead of truly having an understanding that we reap what we sow. A common (phony) shirking of responsibility sentence would be, "If you feel I did such and such, then I am sorry." Sometimes it is followed by, "Sorry you feel that way."

It's not about how one feels, for feelings are not facts. The core solution is to examine how we bring about conflict, and then look to make lists of self-inventory of what actions we took to create the unrest. The key is to realize that we are one hundred percent responsible for whatever transpires.

I revealed a lot in my mea culpa, and did not hold back on anything I felt I could change for the better in me. There was much about the lies too. Now, I'm sure Debby and team were hoping for that big admission she's been seeking all this time. Obviously, since zero of her accusations are true, I would be actually lying if I did say I behaved in those despicable ways. However, the lies of omission can hurt many and it's important that I don't get into a habit of "rating" fibs. Misrepresenting my actions or even a PR campaign to portray me as completely innocent is by all means not being truthful. I spoke to that in the multiple-page cleansing. It was fervent clearings of all that Big G and I could co-create. If it was a heart transplant, here was Doctor Shoe giving recovery its best chance, by disinfecting the area and providing the best space to grow new cells and allow for proper blood flow.

Then, I began to bawl. Big time. Shoulders shaking, the whole bit. I forgot where I was and simply submerged myself in the vibration of the room, truly believing this would be the new beginning we all needed – mostly Michael and Johnny. I looked up and saw my ex-wife starting to cry. Her brother was also wiping away drops from under his eyes. The young guy sitting next to me, who works with Susan helping with my case, starts in too. And, get this, the JUDGE begins to weep!

The same man who was so forbidding the day before was now softened into a different guy entirely.

I believe everyone in attendance that day had a personal clarity moment. After my lawyer finished reading the final page, there was a minute or so of silence. This was no ordinary day downtown. It appeared to hit everyone direct in the heart.

Then Debby and her brother issued brief, cursory, basic and non-specific apologies. Funny. Here I was, finally getting the vindication and expressions of apology I had always demanded, but the words from my ex and brother registered meaningless in my heart. What served me most was my own cathartic exposure. I gained so much more from my honest expression of responsibility and subsequent stated intention than I would ever hope to gain from hearing good words from my ex-wife. Only I hold the key that unlocks the door to personal freedom.

Judge Stevens then began to gently address what he had witnessed. He spoke softly and emotionally, acknowledging the "epiphany" and what it meant to our family. He spoke; "In all my years on the bench and as a lawyer, I have never witnessed anything like this. This was inspirational. I also would like to apologize for my anger yesterday. I thought of you the whole train ride home and I am sorry I was so harsh. I want to protect your children, who are caught in the middle of this, and my passion sometimes gets in the way. I thank you for giving us this moment, and applaud you for doing this for your precious sons. Now, go out and keep this up, and thank your lawyers for the courage it took to do this."

I walked outside the courthouse with a newfound belief. Strange that being accountable for my faults would lead to such joy. It all seemed backwards to what I have been taught as a child as to how to win. For the first time, I truly compre-hended what "sweet surrender" actually is.

Who I am is a mish-mosh of character traits that do not fit into a box the way most would prefer. I cannot be categorized. There is no lid on my ethos, makeup and features. It is ever-evolving, a work in progress, with "progress" being the key to all. My tears, my laughter and even my rage are all signs I am in touch with all that is me. Now, to hide signs of my emotional breakthroughs, such as crying, is living a lie. It is

CRAIG SHOEMAKER

showing people an image that is false. Leah, for some cosmic reason, you and I chose to walk together on this hike through the woods – scary and uncharted. By denying whatever was false, we have been led to discover miracles...our own miracles born within friendship, faith...and yes, even tears.

 Leah De Luca   7/11, 10:22pm

I finished reading a while ago and I am still feeling the spiritual, emotional and physical responses within my being. I am so glad I waited for the right time. My kids went to the mall with friends after we enjoyed dinner together. I was getting antsy waiting for them to go, so that I could fully engulf myself in the experience of receiving your story. When they left, I finished cleaning up, took out the trash, watered the deck plants, changed into my most comfortable shorts and t-shirt, and collapsed on the couch with my laptop. I turned off the TV and for the first time since we began writing one another, I decided to read out loud. Sounds crazy, I'm sure, but knowing that I was about to experience something very special, I had this need to hear what I was reading as I wanted to experience it with as many of my senses as possible.

I didn't only see the words I was reading, I saw "you" in a most wonderful way that I had not yet fully appreciated even after all these months. I didn't only hear myself reading your story aloud, I also heard my own "inner voice" challenging me, questioning whether I too, have been more interested in being perceived by Matt and others as someone who "does the right things," for perhaps self-serving reasons. I heard my inner voice say, *"I am that, I am."*

Your story gave me a "taste" of the sweetness of life that lies ahead for me. More moments of peace with Matt – more forgiveness – more personal accountability. You gave me an appetizer of sorts, an "amuse bouche," leaving me with the aftertaste of "sweet surrender." The surrender FROM conflict, from society's expectations and norms, and most importantly the surrender TO myself. One thing that resonates with me in a very big way is your courage. It is one thing to surrender to self in thought and ideas but quite another to act on it ways that defy the odds, that counter all professional advice, and leave oneself vulnerable to attack from those who would do you harm.

I thank you from my heart, for sharing this with me. I thank the "Big G" for allowing our paths to cross. I thank Mika for bringing out the very best in you. And I even thank your ex-wife, mom, and sister. You once said that the people who brought you so much pain are, in essence, our greatest professors. Perhaps the intermittent pain that lingers in those relationships is a necessary element in keeping you grounded in your life's purpose and keeps you perpetually in the mode and beauty of "surrender."

I find it so interesting that so many people look at Facebook as a waste of time, a shallow way of expressing yourself and sharing mindless chatter with others. Ok, so yes, it is some of that. But wow, if they only knew what was possible. The power of our private exchanges is a divine gift, pure and simple. I am so very grateful for this friendship and I feel that same love and affinity for you. It is not something that can easily be explained or understood. Sometimes I don't understand it myself. And that is quite all right.

CHAPTER ELEVEN

THE COSMIC CLUB OF CATACLYSMIC AND COLOSSAL CONSEQUENCES

Leah De Luca   7/20, 7:46pm

Hey Craig! Needing to connect with you today. Tough day ahead tomorrow – depositions with Matt. Feeling emotional and sad about it. Tried very hard to avoid having depos. I asked Matt several times to consider having us break from this kind of formality and try to work a few things out between the two of us. He is just not willing to do that. As I try to figure out why, the only thing that comes to me is the possibility that he wants the attorneys/legal system to be the "bad guy." If the attorneys dictate what happens, perhaps he feels he is let off the hook? I don't know.

Matt and I spoke several days ago and we had a pleasant conversation, yet, immediately thereafter he shut down again. I have absolutely no idea why. What new thoughts or information came his way to cause the latest end to communication? I am just so worn out. You remember how desperate I was to have him communicate with me all those months ago? Then, once that communication happened, it has been bittersweet.

The communication is what Matt uses to get at my core. I am a communicator. He knows how important that is to me. His control over whether or not that happens on a weekly basis, leads to continued hurt. I keep telling myself that the next time he calls or texts, I will play his game and not respond for days, or at all, leaving *him* to wonder why for the first time. Then I think, no, that's not who I am.

At any rate, looking for kind and peaceful vibes from the West Coast if you have any to throw this way. I am committed to going in to tomorrow with feelings of forgiveness, peace and of course the sweet surrender you spoke of so eloquently. Oh, and going in with an extra large box of tissues. The timing of your beautiful last entry could not have been more perfect. Thank you.

Craig Shoemaker   7/20, 7:58pm

Tough day? I see it as day of progress, fully anticipating a Leah who approaches this seemingly powerful obstacle and walks through it with comfortable confidence and grace. I envision a steady resolve, knowing that nothing at all can happen that cannot be handled. I foresee mindful determination and quiet strength and picture smiles replacing fear-based grimaces and melancholy frowns. No circumstance can take place that can throw you off of your restored sense of self. No person, place, or document can knock you off of your foundation of who you are. Honesty is the marathon winner every time, no matter how fast the perceived foe gets out of the blocks. The worst that can happen will be the best that can happen. More will be revealed and this uncovering will lead to a higher level of consciousness.

You may see him as you never have before and this new-found compassion will guide you through. Out with the old ideas and into your heart goes a deeper understanding of what is in the moment. I see you laughing at how you try to figure him out, a breath of relief from the build up of story you have designed for him.

Tomorrow is your day. Matt has zero to do with the outcome. He will do what he does and his actions or motivations are now meaningless to you. The light chuckles that bubble up are your insides telling you that you are now affirming and confirming that this is all old and of the past. The declarations and courtroom protocol are all symbolic and human, whereas your life now is otherworldly and divine. Lawyers will try to manipulate outcome but you fully know the results are in the hands of an essence and glory that is far beyond the mind of a person set out to win a victory of illusion. You have awareness and deep connection as your tools and you will utilize them to build a new bridge to freedom for you and your entire family. I think your tissues will be used for new purpose, as you cry to acknowledge the presence of the higher source! "Surrender, Dorothy."

Leah De Luca   7/21, 4:32pm

So a quick summary. Depos were scheduled to begin at 10:00 am. I got there an hour early to meet with my attorney and go over things. 10:00 am rolls along. I'm there. My attorney is there. Matt's attorney is there. The court reporter is there. No Matt. 10:30 am, still no Matt. 11:00 am, still no Matt. At one point, his attorney steps out and says Matt called and that he had gotten lost. He finally shows at 11:30 am. No apologies to anyone. It's as if the world has to bow to him and accept his lateness. I closed my eyes for a moment and called on my patience and empathy. I actually tried to make light of the situation by saying hello to him and asking whether he had hit traffic. His response, while barely looking at or acknowledging me, was, "A li'l bit". Not atypical, given lateness has always been the norm for Matt.

I learned today that Matt is unemployed. In comes compassion. My heart does go out to him on this, as I believe Matt wants to be employed. He has never been lazy, but admittedly, I feel a few pangs of frustration and I think to myself that if he's really unemployed, he is the last person who should be late! At any rate, things certainly didn't get things off to a great start. Matt was agitated before anything even started. His dep went first. It lasted for hours. It shouldn't have but his answers to questions were either non-responsive, or he would say he wouldn't answer without consulting counsel at a later time. Or his "half" answers required delving in for more, or constantly rephrasing questions. Even when asked to simply give his opinion on how he felt about certain things, he was defensive, obviously angry at times, and leaving the room several times to get some air.

He shot me some angry looks whenever he didn't like a question that was posed as if to say, "How dare you allow him to ask that!" Much of what he said was truth and that was refreshing. But alas, there were also plenty of exaggerations, omissions, and a couple of flat-out lies. I refused to react with verbal signals and instead, occasionally passed a note to my attorney to clarify or suggest he ask something. Matt made a couple of sarcastic comments about this. He'd stop mid-sentence to say, "I'm waiting to see if she wants to pass you any more notes."

I reminded myself to breathe. Then breathe again. I refrained from doing anything that appeared to agitate him. This helped. Listening to him explain why he felt he should receive alimony made me feel that it had more to do with punishing me than need. He basically said, "Because I was married to her for thirty years." What does that even mean? Again, I witness Matt operating first from fear, and secondarily from anger and I believe this is why alimony is on the table. My deposition was a breeze. I had nothing to hide and it was over very quickly. When it was over, we did talk about possible settlements with real estate and other things but Matt is extremely reluctant to put anything on the table, in terms of what he wants or what he'd accept. The whole day just seemed to piss him off. I wonder again why he didn't accept my numerous offers to work out something less formally between the two of us. In spite of it all, I still plan to make a settlement offer to him next week, in hopes of bringing this all to closure. Sadly, I'm not hopeful because he always seems to think there's something more for him around the corner or that someone is out to get the better of him somehow. Bottom line, the anticipation of today was far worse than the event.

It brings me one step closer to peace so I am thankful for today. I am not afraid anymore of what is to be. What will be, will be, que sera, sera! I just may need to call upon your sanity from time to time. I also remind myself to remember that my situation could be far worse. I call upon my attitude of gratitude as I have so much to be thankful for, your friendship amidst the top of my list.

Craig Shoemaker   7/21, 9:44pm

It still shocks me how much we have in common and in this case, it seems as if you have a male clone of Debby on your hands. The passive-aggressiveness of being late, the coverup lies as to why, the holding all emotionally hostage, and always playing the victim card, which is why they want you to go first, so they can react, instead of simply acting out of a dedicated commitment to common decency. They seem to come with a weather report and we must adjust to their ever-varying emotional temperature changes. It is a game and I want no part of it. So pleased for you that you went through with grace and swiftness. It's what happens when one is genuine and tells the truth. Good for you! I want to give you a big ole hug.

Leah De Luca   8/17, 6:31am

Update. Enjoying every minute with my kids while they are around and gearing up mentally for their departure for college in a few weeks. God, I'll miss them. Been a little tough recently as I ponder what they continue to grapple with in this divorce. I waver from avoiding the topic, to gently prompting discussion on what they need and feel. Hard to know exactly what they need from me. I try to simply be there for them. Sometimes I think I smother them a little and then I back off. No matter their age, I think they need the balance of mother and father, and I'm fairly certain they are not getting everything they need from their dad in his intentional absence and silence. These are the kind of tragic ripple effects of divorce that make you second-guess yourself at times. Enough of that.

I'm gearing up for what promises to be a bit of a stressful week next week. August 23rd is the divorce settlement hearing. I actually submitted a settlement proposal to Matt today through my attorney. But much like my offer to buy him out of our house (he rejected it), I am doubtful that there will be resolution on an overall settlement outside of the formal process/venue. Matt hasn't spoken with me since the depos a couple of weeks ago, though, he did call me late Thursday night last week when I was already asleep. I was a little out of it when he called and said he wanted to talk. When he realized I had been sleeping, he simply asked me to call him back the next day. I did call. No answer. I texted him. Nothing. I emailed him. Still no reply. Really? By the way, I followed your lead and changed Matt's name in my contact list to "Forgive," to understand, to have compassion, to heal.

I had an amazing day with some friends. Yet one acquaintance who was there felt the need to share that she knew Matt had been seeing someone, but that it had not worked out because neither one was ready. Craig, I knew this day would come – the day that I would learn that Matt was or had been seeing someone new. I thought I had completely prepared for this day, in fact, there have been days when I even wished for this to happen. So why does it feel like a kick in the gut? It was like the words were there and I was hearing them but all kinds of thoughts and emotions swirled in my head. On the outside, I tried to appear neutral on the subject and on the inside, I was hurting. Maybe it's symbolic of the end, when in fact the end happened a long time ago I think. Need to work at letting go of the familiar...the familiar is not always good, or peaceful, or happy. It's just familiar. That's all. It's always difficult to let go of what is familiar, even if it's unhealthy. Working on it.

I realize you're on vacation with the fam. So no pressure to respond. Hope you don't mind if I continue using this outlet to express myself. I am in the midst of settlement negotiations with Matt. No idea how it will turn out. Talk with you soon.

Craig Shoemaker   8/17, 11:57pm

Yes! Keep it going. I am on vacay, but you are always important to me. I can totally relate to the kick in the gut. Even with
the difficulties between my ex-wife and me, I get upset when
I hear about a new guy. I think this is natural. My ex has
never lasted more than a few months with anyone. I actually
wish she would. Remember, if the ex is happy, it makes your
life easier. Nothing worse than their reactions to a feeling of
being scorned, so I hope for her sake that she finds someone
to take away the focus from me. I am thinking of hiring a man
to perform the role like a professional actor and date her. This
whole thing, with her running us in and out of court, putting
our sons in hospitals and such has cost me over a million
dollars. If I gave a guy fifty-grand a year, I would be SAVING
money! We can live much freer if they find someone else
to put the nutso shit onto. The jealousy I feel anyway is just
my ego. Remember? Edging God Out. Rejection is Big G's
protection. Hard to believe, but so true...

Leah De Luca   8/20, 10:23am

Things are going better. Just trying to wrap my head around
everything while not skipping a beat at the office or with the
family. Easy, right? Also, still trying to finalize the "deal." We
expect to settle before tomorrow, thus avoiding the hearing.
To "settle" pretty much means for me to give all that I can
possibly give, up front, in exchange for not having to do
spousal support. I'm doing it. I don't need to make a monthly
payment reminding me of what was. I'd really like to move
on with my life. You have no idea how your validation and
understanding of my feelings on the rough issues helps me
to break free from them. I'll touch base again later. Have to
run for work. Your family vacation looks amazing. Your boys
are beaming in the photos – looks like they are having the
time of their lives!

Craig Shoemaker   8/20, 4:16pm

So happy to hear of your very "logical" and reasonable foundation for this settlement. It thrills me to hear you talk in this
way; to have the desire to move on with your life is simply
brilliant and so evolved. You couldn't do any better. You are
basically paying a price for your freedom and there is no
amount of cash that could equal the residual effects of THAT!

What you wrote about the family vacation is correct – smiles & laughs aplenty. This could not happen if not for moving forward with life and that includes acceptance of circumstances that appear to be unfair. It is what it is. I applaud you for moving past it and designing a new dream life for yourself.

Leah De Luca   8/21, 11:56pm

My attorney called me this morning. He said he'd heard from Matt's attorney. Apparently, she told him that her client had "a meltdown" this morning and that he had completely "freaked out" at her. Amazing. Not more than a month ago, Matt's attorney described him as "meek." Bottom line. I SURRENDER! I surrender on more levels than just the financial one. My attorney advises me that even with the latest developments, this is a fair settlement. After grappling with some major feelings of turmoil and unfairness, I quickly surrendered. Funny thing is, when my attorney called Matt's attorney to inform him of my resignation, Matt's response was, "I will accept the offer because I'm tired of fighting." WHAT? I haven't been fighting at all! The only thing I've been doing is offering, giving, offering more, then more, and yet more. I asked for and received NOTHING. Yet, Matt continues to feel threatened, cheated, and that he's 'giving in' to avoid more fighting. You know, I just can't even wrap my head around any of this so I'm not going waste my energy trying.

I feel somewhat validated in that his attorney and mine have witnessed what I lived with for years. Insanity. Unreasonableness. I still feel a little angry that Matt remains expert in getting others to acquiesce and yield to him – to respond and give in because of his meltdowns. But soon, I will no longer be bound by his rules. Read a little excerpt from a book I carry in my pocketbook. It reads, "Nothing can truly be taken from us. There is nothing to lose. Inner peace begins when we stop saying…'I have lost it' and instead say, 'It has been returned to where it came from.' Has your child or spouse died? He or she is returned to where they came from. Have your possessions and property been taken from you? They too, have been returned to where they came from. Perhaps you are vexed because a bad person took your belongings. But why should it be any concern of yours WHO gives your things back to the world that gave them to you? The important thing is to take great care with what you have while the world lets you have it."

I found this interesting. As I confide in a few close family members about some of the terms of the proposed settlement, some perceive that I have "lost" and urge me to "fight" for what is mine. Craig, I want to thank you for teaching me about the beauty and serenity of surrender. Surrender does not mean I'm an idiot but it does mean I choose to let go of certain things in exchange for something much greater. What a process this has been and still is for me!

I have to tell you, following your family travels the past 2 weeks as you revealed them on FB/Twitter has really moved me. While I am navigating through a storm, I have moments in the eye of the storm where I can break to see the beauty, peace and love that comes with surrender. Enjoy your week!

Craig Shoemaker   8/22, 9:18pm

We all hold perceptions about what is "fair" or equitable. I am reading what you wrote about the settlement and... well...feeling angry. Then, I remember my own situation and totally get where you are coming from; to let go of thoughts, ideas and what we believe is "right" is so important to our own serenity. The same goes for all wars and battles, where generations carry on with certain beliefs, concerned with territories and perceptions towards religion or culture, thus spending lifetimes in resentment. When holding onto this crap, it prevents us from being free to live our lives as we were meant to, unencumbered by the nonsense of what is supposed to be "ours," when it is all on loan from "Big G" anyway.

This reminds me of a story. I knew a guy who once had it all. He owned a couple of successful businesses. His gorgeous wife and nice kids helped him run a comedy night club/restaurant business that was thriving in the mid-90s. Then, something happened where he felt wronged and off he went into self-destruction. Ironically, the damage he did to himself was a thousand times greater from his own actions than anything an ex-business associate could have done. He became obsessed with "winning," feeling as if he had been unlawfully misled, and he was hell-bent on beating these guys. He hired lawyers and investigators and anyone else who made their money off of folks in his vulnerable condition. That was when everything in his life went downhill.

First the beautiful wife had an affair and married someone else. Then the kids said bye-bye to this man possessed. No one could stand to be around him and he went into a spiral from which he has still not recovered. My buddy recently told me that our old friend is penniless and practically homeless, due to his choice of fighting, over serenity. Here is a man who had a life I wanted at one time, who turned it all into dust with one stubborn course of action he would not veer from. Incidentally, I am told that he is now suing his former lawyers. Apparently he did not care for their advice.

I mentioned this before, but are you familiar with Borderline Personality Disorder? After studying it and being on the other side of it, I would suggest you check it out, to educate yourself and best prepare for the chaos that ensues when it is rearing its head. It is as if you are in a roller coaster operated by a drunken carny. You are locked in and screaming for help, as they turn your life upside down. The part about Matt's attorney made me laugh. Debby goes through people like that. It always begins well, with her kissing ass to look good, complimenting them to gain favor and lure 'em into her manipulative world. I have heard from her mouth numerous times when she has a new lawyer, or a therapist is hired, "You are amazing. I don't know how you do it." Then with a phony chuckle and nod in my direction, "Are you sure you can handle a high-conflict couple like us?"

They are all allies but the moment they do not comply one hundred percent, they become sworn enemies. The same ones who are complimented and praised, are now deemed incompetent and (worse) criminal. Do not cross the border on the borderline. Borderline is a bitch, and the worst aspect of the Borderlines' issues is that they will NEVER seek or get help. No matter how bad it looks for them, do not expect any kind of accountability. As you and I know though, it is our internal, peace-guided suggestions that will lead to victory for us. My son says his mom only wants to win at all costs but it is only her "idea" of winning, which includes never admitting wrong or apology. Borderlines' terms include trying to convince everyone else that you are crazy, to put all off the scent of who is actually and hugely insane.

As long as our map is co-written with a higher source, we will be led to the Promised Land. It is a matter of priority, and I am glorified in hearing what you have found to be most important – letting go and allowing a transformation to take place. You are making space for something you have not experienced yet.

Welcome. Welcome to the Cosmic Club of Cataclysmic and Colossal Consequences! Up here, we breathe only the finest air. We have enlivened our taste buds that now savor the treats we have previously only sniffed. In this space, love has no bounds. We do not allow others to bring us into their lonely and tired space but we take off for a journey to places we can feel in our core.

And our ex-spouses are not on the VIP list…

Leah De Luca   8/31, 11:59pm

You just make me smile, seriously. I just got back home from a great trip. Spent some quality time with my friend Marianne, her daughter, and one of my daughters. We went to North Carolina where Marianne's daughter is in school. She proudly cooked us an amazing meal, and then we all hung out listening to music and sipping wine.

My daughter and I left on Sunday for her college up north. I helped her move in and get situated. Love her housemates. They're great and I really enjoy getting to know her friends. As we moved her in, we ran into several parents who were also moving their kids back in. Maybe it was my imagination but, everywhere I looked, there seemed to be a mom AND a dad. I wondered if she noticed the same thing? Maybe I'm overly sensitive about this. But as I told you recently, my heart goes out to my kids, as I believe they are in pain from the intentional lack of contact from their dad.

Found out today that the court date to finalize the divorce will be moved into October. I am feeling a little anxious about the lack of momentum in getting this all behind me. The final court date, the sale of the house, the movement to somewhere new. None of this changes the reality of what is happening but it's all symbolic for me. I feel a pull and tug sometimes and feel I can't totally break free from some of the paradigms that hold me back, until some of these milestones are achieved. So, I am waiting patiently for the universe to have its way with me, still surrendering to my life. What a journey!

CHAPTER TWELVE
STUMBLING UPON GRACE

Leah De Luca   9/24, 7:48pm

Hey there! Have some catching up to do. I spent a little bit of time, amidst trying to finish packing up my house, reading some older entries between us. Amazing and uplifting, difficult and eye opening, inspiring... brings out so many emotions in me. I truly have to print out this entire dialogue from the beginning and retrace the steps that brought me to today. I am amazed how I have forgotten much of what we shared with one another, and how powerful it has been. How one entry here or there got me through some very difficult times this past year. I enjoy reading your FB posts about fun and love with family and friends.

Craig Shoemaker   9/25, 7:11pm

Leah, your joy is practically bursting through the page. I am so happy for you. Also, I am honored to have shared your expedition alongside you this past year. Life is not easy, divorce is not easy, yet somehow, our darkest days are never so dark when we have someone to share them with.

Incidentally, I talked to one of "us" the other day and shared this amazing experience I'm, having with you, as well as my impulse to turn this into a novel. You may have heard of this man, because his work can certainly be deemed as otherworldly; the space in which you and I now choose to exist. He is "one of us." By that I mean that (long ago) this incredible man chose to rise above the incessant teasing and naysayers, and listen to his creator. He was shunned, bullied and beaten, but nothing could stop the deep consciousness that yearned to be let out.

His name is Paul Williams. You might know him from the countless songs that are a large part of our culture. He is an Oscar winner, Grammys – the whole shebang. Wrote songs like "Rainy Days & Mondays" for the Carpenters and "Evergreen" for Streisand. He even penned "Rainbow Connection" for the Muppets! Anyway, we golfed the other day as we have been meaning to get together for a day of golf for years but couldn't make it happen. He's busy, I'm busy, whatever it was and we could not make it work. Until last week, he and I kinda knew one another on a peripheral level, as well as having a mutual respect as artists.

A few days ago, we nailed down a time and place. I get there late, having had to deal with another ex-wife carnival of emotional rides. I was out of sorts and panting when I see Paul calmly hitting balls on the range. He has a smile on his face and he is preparing to be the architect of a wonderful day, no matter what the circumstances. And we did. Just the two of us, perfect and meant to be.

It took me a few holes to wash off the goo, but a groove was found both on the course and also inside the cart. We rapped about everything you can think of, from our all-too-similar childhoods, to how we both found ultimate love late in life and after some disastrous tries. I even got to hear the inside scoop on the history of songs that are a huge part of my growing up! Pretty neat...But the one aspect of our day has to do with you, who I feel is a member of the elite club Paul and I belong to – Thinkers & Believers in Higher Purpose. I talked a lot to Paul about our non-planetary relationship, and he was very moved by our letters of significance here on Facebook. I described the depth and meaning and subsequent healing felt from this back-and-forth dialogue through private messaging. He gave me that twinkling smile I used to see when he was a guest so many times on the *Tonight Show* with Johnny Carson, and shooting me a knowing grin he said, "I have the title...*Gracebook.*"

I talked to some about the word "grace," and all believe it to be a Christian term. As you know, religion is not my thing, as I see how much harm it has done to humanity, however the word "spirituality" is something I fully embrace. In my world, the word "grace" has a different meaning than anything religious, for it simply means finding that space of goodwill, acceptance and peace. An atheist, agnostic or anyone from any background should have a goal of grace. It's just a good way to live, especially without the dogma. Why attach a group to something we can achieve as individuals?

 Leah De Luca   9/26, 9:04am

As for the exchanges with the great Paul Williams and the great Craig Shoemaker, all I can say is that I am humbled to have even been a part of that conversation. And while I'm not convinced that I am completely fit just yet for entry into that elite club you speak of, I know in my heart that is where I belong. This is where my heart pulls me...and that is the road less traveled on my journey.

Come to think of it, I have always loved the "Rainbow Connection" song. More than ever, I find myself smiling over the lyrics...

"Rainbows are visions, but only illusions, and rainbows have nothing to hide. So we've been told and some choose to believe it. I know they're wrong, wait and see. Someday we'll find it, the rainbow connection. The lovers, the dreamers and me."

Craig Shoemaker   9/30, 9:12 am

I have an I-Phone now. It has "Siri," a woman's voice who dials up pretty much anything you ask for. I spoke into my phone, "Call my ex-wife." She responded, "Have you thought this one through?"

You know I'm joking but one thing that is true is how I still respond to women's harsh judgment. I swear, even with a mechanical voice speaking to me, I can hear the critical tone from when I make a wrong turn in my car. It seems like I can glean sarcasm from Siri when she says with her eyes rolling, "Re-routing."

Ok, I know it is fresh and you have stated that you can't even think about dating yet... but I have a hunch. You know how our whole year-long dialogue began with me listening to an inner voice? I am an "energy guy," and many of my moves are inspired by feeling certain vibrations from people, after which I act accordingly. That is, when I am centered. To attract what we want, it takes spiritual fitness. If someone wants a hot body, they work out at the gym. You want brains, you might say, "Hey, I like to do the *New York Times* cross-word too!" Well one thing I know to be true is that Mika's and my beautiful relationship is due to the fact that we know it is bonded in the vibration of the divine. If we are off-kilter, it only means there have been fewer higher source workouts. Time to do some Prayer Pilates!

Since the moment you and I began writing to one other, I have been compelled to suggest ways for you to experience a new system for living and loving; one which will lead to something you have basically sought but did not attain, in 30 years of marriage. I have felt all along that a light-hearted and kind man will come into your life, if you are willing to let go of the old concepts that led you to dark places. Well, guess what? Your new buddy Craig has had another strong urge and this time it is specific. I have a great track record setting people up and actually fixed up four marriages in one year, and eight or nine matrimonial hookups over my lifetime. These days I'm an ordained minister. Been marrying couples in what I call, "HaHa-trimony," making sure they realize that a sense of humor is KEY to sustaining a relationship. However, in this case I don't think I need to submit my matchmaking resume. I know you trust me and respect me.

With that in mind, I am suggesting that you go on a date with a man who shares much in common with you. He too is recently separated after 30 years of an abusive relationship. Jack was married to someone I've known since grade school. His ex treated him in a similar fashion to how our exes treated us. Also similar to you is his compelling need to move on in life. He backed that up by sacrificing (surrendering) so much of his hard- earned money to his ex, wanting to get it over with without fighting her. Sound familiar?

He is a good and kind man; the type of man I spoke of you finding, once you clear the path to share the road. You both deserve better and my inklings say that (at the very least) it will be good for both of you to experience true kindness and respect from the opposite sex, even if but for a few dates.

Here's the thing – I have known this friend since kindergarten, so he is "FULLY VETTED." I shared milk, toy trains and a cot with this guy! You don't have to go through a trust-gathering process, or show up on a date and find a dude who used another profile picture. (By the way, a fan of mine showed me a Match.com profile of a guy in Texas who used MY photo to represent him! Too funny. I was no big hit looks-wise when I was single…so good luck, buddy! Anywho…Jack's general value and moral system is as good as it gets and he possesses a great deal of integrity. So, with your permission I will give him your number so you can go on a date. Not saying he's Brad Pitt and maybe not your physical type. He is much different than how you describe Matt. He is subtle and very kind, as well as generous and thoughtful. You have nothing to lose though, and my sense is that there's a lot to gain from going out with someone who has the ability to do something to you that you have been craving for a lifetime – appreciate you for who you truly are.

Leah De Luca   9/30, 6:10 pm

Craig, are you crazy?! I can't be dating just yet. Don't I need time to grieve? The ink isn't even dry on the divorce papers.

Craig Shoemaker   9/30, 9:31 pm

I'm going to break our chain and call you by phone on this one. I know you trust me, and I'd like to talk this through. Besides, with all this writing, I'm going to have Carpal Tunnel Syndrome!

CHAPTER LUCKY THIRTEEN

ONE YEAR LATER...

Craig Shoemaker 8/3, 2:30pm

I know I'm always speaking of visions but now I just can't believe this one...how it played out, that you are madly in love with my fix-up a year later! Nostradamus couldn't have predicted this from the way it all began. Leah, to see you down the Jersey shore with Jack was a delight on so many levels. It was great for you to be able to spend time with our family and Mika simply adores you so much. It is hard to comprehend that this is the first time we've spent time together, since we became so intimate and revealing with each other over the past year. It was so nice of you to baby-sit the kids too, while Mika got some (much needed) alone time to surf. I guess you kinda feel like you know us all already, but now the face-to-face brings it alive. Your glow is an amazing thing to be around.

When I hung with you and Jack a few months ago in NY, I came back home and expressed how joyful I felt at seeing you two so happy. And I can't believe another of my matchmaking efforts seems to have scored! This trip, however, my melt was even more felt, as I observed you and my "fixup" simply living in such comfort and happiness. Even our other friends who witnessed your loving connection, expressed to Jack how wonderful it is to see him be able to be himself, without being berated or cut down as he was in his marriage. I know you and Jack talk often about "where you came from" in your years of compromise and abuse but from another view, I can tell you it rings bells in my heart to see you two together.

Mika has expressed her delight in meeting you too. She picks up such a great vibe, and enjoyed getting to know the one who occupied her husband so much for a year! It's as if a character in a play came alive. She had tried to picture what you were like. It was fun for me to see how much she dug you. And that you were able to so easily adjust to Jackson and he to you is a testament to who you are.

I cannot and will not predict the future of you and Jack but suffice to say, it is something to behold when I hear him speak of you and you of him. This guy spent his entire adult life jumping through hoops to please his spouse and the results were disabling. I recognize this because I came from it, with constant attempts to please the ones we chose to dictate how we felt about ourselves. But unfortunately, the pure love will not take place in those cases of the self-involved. Now, we get to be free to be self-"E"volved, and embrace one another in support of a new way of living we deserved all along.

I told 2 of my sons the other day to never get in relationship with scorekeepers. "What's a scorekeeper, Dad?" says Johnny. "Well, it's a person who keeps tabs on what you do for them and uses their version of totals against you. And just know this boys, you will never have victory. They own the scoreboard. The field is all built to their specs and they even get the fans on their side. They don't play fair, so don't even bother joining the league. With few morals and little good faith, they will lie to be the winner, leaving you perplexed and dismayed. The best thing you can do is move on. Leave. Just don't play their game anymore and they will find someone else to do battle with." I think the boys got it. I feel for them, since I also come from this parental alienation by an extreme narcissist. It is sad but they are resilient, and have their own road to trudge.

Leah, I am beyond happy that you can now be matched up with someone who sees you divinely. It's all we need. Your authentic self deserves to be recognized, heard and loved. Mine does too and I cannot fathom how I spent so many years in the discovery process. I guess it takes what it takes – "God's a slow mother fucka!" This has been quite an odyssey for all of us. I think it's just the beginning…love you!!!

CHAPTER FOURTEEN

MY MAN, "EPILOGUE"

Leah De Luca 8/5, 9:34am

Craig, I hope this message finds you, Mika and the boys in good health and in a great place. It's hard to believe another year has passed. My state of "being" is barely recognizable from what it was on that bleak day when I reached out to you a couple of years ago to let you know what was about to unfold in my life. All the foreshadowing in the world couldn't have convinced me back then, of the beauty and grace that lay ahead. I feel so happy, so full of peace, so grateful. Where do I begin?

Almost a year ago, you gently invited me to me to connect with someone that you knew from your childhood, and still know today – your friend, Jack. Someone who you told me was a very kind and good person, someone going through a divorce as well, and whose journey over the past many years had ironic similarities to mine. It took a few phone calls and a little bit of convincing, as you well know. I had spent the better part of a year navigating a difficult divorce, and had not opened my heart yet to allowing new people "in," or scarier yet, to the idea of dating in middle age. As I said to you many times, I yearned for and hoped that one day I might find the kind of relationship grounded in authentic love that you have with Mika...but I meant "one day," not just now. Because if finding that authentic love meant opening my heart and being vulnerable, well again, maybe "not just yet."

I had internal doubts, I conveniently looked for obvious excuses: "My divorce was just finalized"... "I have to focus on myself, and my work and my kids right now"...I just wasn't sure I was ready. But as usual for you, you had a way of breaking through. You wouldn't let me get away with pushing this idea aside. You once again lovingly nudged me to go outside of my comfort zone. I was holding back due to fear – fear of what agreeing to meet a guy actually meant. Fear of starting over, and more importantly, fear of opening my heart to someone. Someone once said, *"Be careful who you give your heart to. Because when you give your heart to someone, you also give them the power to hurt you."*

The what-ifs kicked in big time. I remember shaking my head as if to snap out of a trance and thinking, *C'mon, Leah, this is just meeting someone, for God's sake. Don't give this so much importance – it doesn't mean anything, I meet people every day through work, etc., so just go with it.* But this felt different – I have no idea why. I trusted you. And I am so very grateful for what has manifested in my life. True to your promise, Jack is a wonderful human being who, for whatever reason, you sensed would become a dear friend and possibly much, much more to me.

When we began spending time together, we worried because we did what any professional would say not to do when meeting someone new after divorce, and that is, we talked about our exes and our experiences with them. We TALKED and talked ad nauseam about it. You are NOT supposed to do this, right? But for us, it was like a continuing journey of healing and supporting one another while confronting and tackling feelings of anger, compassion, guilt, sadness, forgiveness, and love. I remember sitting quietly with Jack one night and he turned to me and whispered, "Do you still love Matt?" I hadn't shed a tear in months, as most all of the turmoil of the divorce was behind me, but this simple question made my emotions flow like a volcanic eruption. I cried, for the first time I believe, in front of Jack. "Yes," I confided to him. "In spite of everything, I will most likely always love Matt (albeit a different kind of love). He is the father of my kids and I acknowledge a great and continuing sadness that I wasn't able to make my marriage work and keep a wonderful family together for my kids."

Jack didn't feel threatened. He had no reason to. He just listened, as he always does, and he loved me in his spiritual, quiet way. He understood and perhaps identified with these feelings. Over the ensuing months, we had numerous exchanges and personal revelations like this. I drew out his feelings and he did the same for me – we did it for each other, on countless occasions.

I recall we spent a romantic evening under the stars, this last summer, on the rooftop of a building overlooking the city of New York. We talked about our doubts and fears about what was clearly becoming a much stronger connection between us. We were both very scared of what was happening. It was too fast. It didn't make sense. Were we on the rebound? It seemed too good to be true. We are both so different from one another's exes, in every sense; physical, spiritual, intellectual. We should be playing the field, right? We talked about people in each of our lives who often gave us their "view" of the world. Some were happy and encouraging about what was evolving, others were cynical, and yet others were downright negative about what they sensed was happening; warning us of impending danger and all the pitfalls of what a serious new relationship might mean.

Jack kept telling me he wasn't even really sure about what he was afraid of with our deepening and wonderful relationship but he acknowledged that he had fear. I pressed to better understand what he meant. He quoted Marianne Williamson: ***"Our deepest fear is not that we are inadequate. Our deepest fear is that we are powerful beyond measure."***

Tears flowed from his eyes. In acknowledging that we do in fact have "power beyond measure," he realized that he was more fearful of our relationship succeeding, than he was of it failing! A successful relationship had all kinds of implications – and he talked about his tendency, up until that night, to "hold back" in his true feelings for me. To this day, he tells me that at that moment, on the roof…is the moment he knew he fell in love with me. It was one of the most beautiful experiences. It had built up over many months, in the most beautiful, gradual way of getting to know someone. We have spent the last year peeling back the onion together, and there are still so many layers. Some of our "digging" and time together occasionally brings one or both of us to the point of tears; beautiful tears of awareness, love, and yes, sometimes fear. Craig, I am experiencing love on a level that is unrecognizable to me. It is beyond the physical, in fact, the physical has evolved from something much greater and deeper.

 Craig Shoemaker   8/6, 2:30pm

I totally relate. Today, as I chip away at the man-made creation of Craig, I gain a better understanding of what my purpose and destiny are. I did not come to this planet to be put into a convenient package that will please others. I am here to unfold the unique magnificence that I am. A mother at Johnny's school came up to me, upset at a Facebook post I wrote about my ex and her recent shenanigans. I guess people think you are an oppressor when you are a man, especially a pretty successful one, because it appears to be a bullying, with the powerful male dominating everyone around him and sycophants allowing the domination to take place, fearful to speak up. But I assured her that I am motivated by one thing – I wish to share hope with others, so they know all will be okay, even when it seems bleak.

As this transformation is taking place, I find the road is narrow and getting even smaller. I used to almost pride myself on knowing so many people. Now my goal is to cut loose those who suck the goodness out of the room. For most people, it is easier to take the path of least resistance. My journey may now attract a select few, the highest quality of people, while some old relationships go on hiatus. Mika is the ultimate gift from the highest source, to show me I'm on to something. Just as when someone laughs at a joke I tell, I now "get" the humor of G, even if I'd like to occasionally walk out on his show!

Leah De Luca   8/10, 10:20pm

Craig, this past year has also been one of the most fun and uplifting years of my life. Jack and I have done so much together, experienced so much. The arts, theatre, museums, musicals, workshops, religious and spiritual gatherings, even listening to audio-books with ear-buds through a splitter while sitting side-by-side on the beach – squeezing one another's hands as we can both appreciate a relevant or important part of what we are hearing. Long walks, dinners, and yes, comedy shows! We are becoming best friends, loving and appreciating the time we are blessed to have together. We have made new friends together as well, and still enjoy the old friends too.

Not long ago, we attended a "Forgiveness" Workshop together. The workshop was provided by a woman who has been a client of Jack's for many years but she was someone he really knew only peripherally. He sent me an email from her foundation a few months ago, advertising this "forgive-ness workshop," and did so sort of as an "FYI." I immediately suggested that we go. Before I get into that, I want you to know more about this amazing spirit and human being, Jack's client – Mariah Fenton. Mariah suffers from ALS and has defied all odds, in living with the disease for over 20 years. She is one of the longest living survivors of ALS (if not THE longest living), and when she was originally diagnosed, she was given only two years to live. The years and disease have since taken their toll on her. She is confined to a wheelchair now and depends largely on her husband Ron, her sons and crew to help her not only with her foundation and life's work but with the simple, day-to-day activities that you and I take for granted. Her son is currently making a documentary about her and the service she's accomplished in her lifetime, while at the same time battling her disease. So where am I going with this?? One might think – What kind of workshop could this woman possibly give with such a handicap? She can barely speak without someone to help translate. Couple this with Jack and me taking part in something so personal and unfamiliar together, and well, you can see why the build-up is so important.

We went, with somewhat low expectations. We enjoyed the car ride through Pennsylvania's countryside to the location of the workshop. As always, we traveled with no need to be entertained by radio. We are one another's entertainment. We are generally never at a loss for words (though Jack tells me most would say he is not a talker), and when we aren't speaking, we are holding hands and/or just "being." Experts have described a unique form of communication that infant/ young twins sometimes develop – a language that no one else understands but which bonds them very specially. This is what I feel when Jack and I are still. Hard to describe. At any rate, we arrived at the workshop where we found about 150+ others, who we guessed were sorting through their own forgiveness issues. This was a 4-hour workshop and not knowing if we were "full-in," we decided we would sit towards the back, giving ourselves the opportunity to sneak out, if that turned out to be necessary.

Things began with Mariah's loving and encouraging insights about forgiveness. Each person was challenged to look internally at what had brought them to this place, on this day. Some offered bits of their stories, some extremely powerful – one man revealed that his step-son had murdered his wife. He was there trying to make sense out of his life and how to deal with what his step-son had done. I thought ...And I'm here...why??? To make sense of my divorce? Seemed trivial to say the least. Still, I listened.

I scribbled notes that I maintain today, with some of Mariah's words as she struggled to articulate them. She said, "Forgiveness is to release resentment and any desire for retribution. It does not mean you condone the behavior, it means you have done the work of releasing anger in a non-destructive way. You have arrived at an understanding at how this person, given his or her history, could have (or is still) behaving in this way. That you have explored deeply and put yourself in his or her shoes, and that you have forgiven the other for his or her numb, arrogant, unskilled, or abusive choice(s). That you know that in you too, lies a lack of skill, arrogance and apathy sometimes. Outright cold and meanness – does anyone not have those disabilities? As humans, we are capable of atrocities."

Wow. It felt as if our year-long conversation on Facebook was being revealed before my eyes, in high speed, kind of like your life flashing before your eyes on your deathbed, as some have described. Reverse to the days of learning of more of Matt's "unskilled and arrogant choices" that finally led to our divorce filing...fast forward to my pain and anger and desire for his accountability...then to his desire to punish me, to shut down. The battles and the ultimate war that were waged, and in the end, no one really wins. The divorce, as you well know, had its ups and downs and in the end, surrender was the word of the day. It allowed me peace and to move on. But little did I realize that as much as I said throughout our writings that I had forgiven Matt, I am here to say that this may not have been entirely accurate. Moreover, I still had not forgiven myself.

And so the workshop continued. At Mariah's direction, I drew a forgiveness bulls-eye on a piece of paper, writing down the names of people in my life whom 1) I have been able to give unconditional forgiveness (in the center) 2) whom I am in the process of forgiving (in the middle) and 3) whom I have not or cannot forgive (in the outermost circle). I won't tell you where I included Matt and myself, but suffice it to say, neither were in the "inner circle." Several group exercises and two hours later, Jack and I found ourselves more entrenched in what was happening. It was break time and if we were going to leave, now would be the opportune time. No, something kept us there.

After break, it was announced that Mariah would work with one member of the audience directly. The way in which this person would be selected would be a draw, for which our names had been printed and entered. I leaned over to Jack and whispered, "This is one lottery I do NOT want to win." As I finished uttering those words, Ron Gladis, Mariah's husband, opened the paper he pulled from the container and announced, "Do we have Leah in the room?"

I wanted to run out of the room, but called on my inner-Craig, knowing that there was a reason this was happening.

What followed was so surreal – a one-on-one session with this remarkable woman, in front of the entire audience. I was asked to share who I wanted to forgive and what I wanted to be forgiven for. Someone in the room was asked to volunteer to take on the persona of Matt. I had the chance, working with Mariah, to literally talk through my reasons and desires for forgiveness between me and Matt. As beautiful music played in the background, Matt (i.e., the person who played his role) and I walked toward one another, arms open wide, acknowledging one another's past hurts, expressing our need to forgive and be forgiven. As I write this, I can't convey the power of this session. I cried like a baby, and as I did so the entire room began to wipe away tears. They too, were thinking of the reasons they had come; the people they needed to forgive or be forgiven by. Powerful. I turned my head to see Jack, who was weeping. While a total stranger was in front of me "playing" Matt, I only saw the real Matt. I saw a beautiful, loving man who was forgiving me, and I forgave him with all of my heart. When we finally reached one another after walking across the room, we embraced. I closed my eyes, tears flowing like a river, imagining this was the REAL Matt in my arms. I could barely let go.

Having this experience, and more importantly, having it with Jack and having him see me in such a vulnerable state, was a gift beyond measure. He was so proud of me and it only made us closer. Suffice it to say, I do not know what lies ahead for Jack and me but I know that he will ALWAYS be an important part of my life. I know that I am blessed beyond measure to have him in my life. I know that he is a spirit that I love and admire. I am blessed. I am grateful. And I thank you, from my heart of hearts. xoxo

---

Craig Shoemaker   9/1, 3:49pm

Of course you were chosen! HaHa. Love it…and really dig what you were taught in the seminar. I just spent a weekend with Jack and he certainly is one happy dude. Since he knows all about our exchanges and that there might be a book out of all this, I now teasingly call him "Epilogue."

So glad Jack was able to join us our annual guy getaway with the old neighborhood pals, especially considering our buddy Rob's difficult health condition. We really needed the comic relief! On this trip, one of our crew, Stewy, ate sweet "treats" Rob brought with him, chowing down like it was his last meal. They were actually not desserts per se, but Rob's medicine for his chemo – POT COOKIES! Then clueless, stoned Stewy begins talking like a guy shot up with Novocain speaking in ancient tongues. He thought he was communicating with us but we couldn't understand a friggin' word he said. Cannabis doesn't mix as well with a middle-aged man's brain. He turned into a bumbling idiot…much to our delight!!

I look forward to your impending visit with Epilogue, to our home in California. I'm so glad I moved here years ago. After all, if I still lived in Philly, this crazy, New Age shit would have never happened!! LOL Love you! Craig

THE NEVER
ENDING AFTERWARD

Leah, it has been a while. You might be out of sight but your essence travels far. Can you believe how much has happened to us?! It amazes me, how when one simply steps out of the way, surrenders, allowing a source of solid intention to do its job, the results are more amazing than if it were up to our own minimal thinking. Even with Mika, I sometimes see her become hyper-focused on something, as it appears she won't be happy unless she gets it. She researches, puts things through full appraisal process, always trying different methods to achieve what she thinks she wants.

Actually, since I am more the opposite, fly-by-the-seat-of-my-pants guy, I often laugh at my little nerd when she's immersed in her latest project. One of the things that attracted me to her to begin with was when she had set her sights on opening a teahouse that would double as a library of sorts, which taught environmental sustainability. Mika also decided to bag any dreams of becoming an actress (praise the heavens for THAT!), and concentrate on working behind the scenes. So, she became a union electrician on movie sets, and on some really big feature films to boot! She will put the same amount of passion into learning more about her vagina through Kegel workouts, finding the best place to put our electronic waste or creating a four-year-old birthday party that rivals Gymboree or Chuck E Cheese. At this last shindig for Jackson, all the kids had home-made superhero costumes to put on and she took their photos upon this cityscape on a dark sheet, making it look like they were flying over buildings on a starry night.

Mika coming to my life is the perfect, and I mean perfect, show of what happens when I define my higher purpose, repeat it over and over, take consistent actions of integrity, then get the hell out of the way. I'm reminded every day of how anyone can have true love, and that you don't have to "work" at it. The connectedness is just there. No forced classes or groups on how to get what you "need" from a relationship. Simply water our personal, metaphoric soil every day, and provide plenty of light. Be kind, gentle and loving. Then, voila! The most beautiful garden only Mother Nature could design. Come to think of it, Mika's full name means "River Lotus" in Japanese. It's even in her email address. I had not thought of its significance until now. She flows with the steady calm and sound of a beautiful body of water, with the soft and striking beauty of a Lotus flower. I can look at Mika every day and be blown away by my feelings for her. Yup, she is the Law of Attraction incarnate. I am the luckiest man in the world.

One blind spot or lack of completion she seems to have had for quite some time, is her wish to have another child, specifically a girl. She is the best step-mom imaginable to Michael and Johnny, and an amazing mother to Jackson. The 2 older boys, though not her blood, even call her Mama. We've been doing a "Gratitude List" at the dining room table for all these years, and recently added, "What I love about you," to our Monday dinners. To listen to the boys speak so candidly, lovingly and eloquently about my wife is actually breathtaking. It often brings chills when I step back and observe us all together; playing, kayaking, hiking, putting puzzles together, acting out Charades – the whole shebang. During holiday season at our house, the gift is in the presence, not the presents, as the joy goes up a notch to "11."

Yet a wee bit of sadness peeks out from my wife's easy demeanor. There are a lot of "sausages" in this Shoemaker clan. Even though I grew up in a home with only females, as fate would have it, it's all boys in this house. Our dog Zoey might be a girl, but even she is a "King" Charles Cavalier. It is time to add a feminine touch to the mix.

Several years ago, Mika shared with me that she has (since the age of eleven) believed she would some day have a daughter and that she had picked a name for her: Chloe. I told her: "I'm more of an Emily guy but I can go with that." A week or so after our conversation about Mika's vision, Michael excitedly approached me. He was 11 at the time. These two have always been strangely bonded, even sharing the same birthday, as well as Michael looking half-Asian as Mika is. He says, "Dad, I had this really vivid dream. You and Mika are going to have a baby. And her name is "Chloe."

Leah, my first inclination was to assume that my wifey had spoken to him too about her decades-long plan but no, she had not said a word to him. So, when she did get preggers a year or so later, the two of them started calling the belly "Chloe," figuring this was meant to be. I kept faux-yelling at them to stop that, and see if they could match up again with a boy's name, just in case their ethereal bonding was off this time.

CRAIG SHOEMAKER

Nope. They refused to bend their solid beliefs. They went on calling the growing fetus, Chloe.

On a Monday, Mika and I go to the doctor for ultrasound and so on. The OBGYN, which always sounds like a Star Wars character to me, asks if we want to know the gender. My cocky wife says she already knows it is a girl. Pointing to the screen the all-knowing Obi-Wan replies, "That's no girl." What?!! You mean these two have been calling my son a girl's name for three months??!!

I told em both to call their psychic hotline and get crackin' on finding a match on a boy's name. The next day I flew to New York to have dinner with an old friend and Mika flew to Philly around the same time. I scooted from my friend's place, got in the rental car, and drove down the Jersey Turnpike to rendezvous with my wife. I answer my cell. It's Michael. "Dad, I came up with the perfect name. You were married by the water in Maui. The name is also kinda Hawaiian/Asian. How bout Kai, spelled K-A-I?" I said sarcastically, "KAI?? I'm on my way to my hometown. He would get his ass kicked in Philly with a name like KAI!"

Yes, Leah, I often forget we are in a different day and age than the one I grew up in, with old-school beatings like the ones I endured for being a bit different or "unique." That thought aside, I met up with Mika in the City of Brotherly Love and she was beaming, expressing to me that she'd gone through a book of a thousand baby names and she'd found one. As I said, always thorough like a "spiritual scientist," she scoured through pages of names and their derivations, arriving at the top choice that resonated with her. I said with Philly attitude, "Well, it won't match with your meta-physical doppelganger THIS time! Michael called me on the way here, all excited about a name he picked. 'KAI!' How the hell did he come up with… honey…you're looking at me strange…what's up?"

Mika is showing all signs of a woman having some sort of internal electric shock. She turns to me with engorged goose bumps, "Oh my God…let me not tell you, let me show you." Like a magic trick, she pulls out a piece of paper with a name handwritten at the top, "Kai." You gotta be kidding me!!!

It was truly a strange, cosmic twist to our ever-surprising and evolving tale. But I still kept contemplating the reaction of telling my conservative mother that her grandson would be named Kai. This was when we were somewhat getting along with my mom. Can you believe I was still allowing her harsh judgments of me to affect my decisions? I knew she would purse her lips and try to feign approval of the name but rather than risk that, we named him Jackson, his middle name being Kai.

My mom doesn't even know this grandson, still only speaking to Michael and Johnny through clandestine arrangements with my ex, while completely ignoring our youngest son (and Mika as well). Mom would rather take this path of hurting so many, than sit down for an hour with me to talk things through. She and my sister have chosen to foster a relationship with my ex-wife, who to this day spreads the most disgusting lies about their own flesh and blood. Sure, they make excuses about how they perceive my actions but not sure how they justify punishing a child or even Mika. One would think a family would celebrate my wife, knowing how much joy she gives me. Plus, she is great to the boys, who are not hers. Sick stuff, and I cannot keep fishing in a toxic pond or I'll get food poisoning.

You can easily see the benefit Jackson has by being raised in this balanced home. Frankly, although they've been subjected to a helluva lot of upheaval, I'm so proud of the young men Michael and Johnny have become too. They deal with their angst in different ways, but they are really, really good kids. Mika, however, never got her Chloe, and it is painful to see her trials in this regard.

As you know, she had a miscarriage, which we both (mistakenly) believed was a result of the anxiety/pain felt in being attacked so much by Debby. I think Mika shares an unfortunate technique in dealing with such (seemingly) unprovoked mayhem – shut the body down. Mika had two miscarriages and was so distraught. But you know me, the hopeful guy whose empathic intuition rules the day; I had to step in.

I began to offer my feelings and suggestions to Mika as to what I felt would assist her in a healing, and hence perhaps bring in a baby she wanted so much. At its best, even this "book" of ours was written with one key technique – letting go. Allow the otherworldly plan to unfold and get the hell out of the way instead of trying to manipulate results. Be cognizant of being good to self and others. The outcomes will be what they are meant to be – but the plan we hold must be in conjunction with spirit. As much as we have invited in turmoil, send out the request for the presence of the presence. Put out only a message of pure love and it will be answered in ways seemingly unimaginable. Yes, sweet surrender is called for again, even if it first tastes bitter.

I gently leaned on Mika to change it up a bit. Put more focus on not having a baby necessarily, but into building a safe space for the child to be. My environmentally conscious girl was having a tough time with the ecosystem footprint in her own home. So, she set out to change it up, going to classes and a getaway retreat, as well as making clear decisions to laugh more. I cannot say it enough – we all need to LAUGH more! It is so incredibly healing to have hearty giggles and guffaws. Mika and I set the intention to find more funny in our lives. It worked.

A palpable shift in energy took place. Mika's worry began to leave her body. Her smile became wider. Now THIS is a space any baby would want to hang in! Mika also told the universe she was fine with what we had, that we didn't really need a new child, and that we were in acceptance & gratitude for what we had. At first, this may have been faked, but eventually it was absolute. The final sign of getting it was my incredible wife being brave enough to sell all of Jackson's baby stuff, showing Big G she truly was letting go.

We stopped "trying" to have a baby. No more fertility treatments or appointments. No more following the ovulation clock. She dropped the analytical and began the possible. No more human doing – now back to human being. Being in the now, being true to what is real, being in the awesome communion with a higher source.

Well, I guess this hocus-pocus shit really works. One day, I had one of my hunches. Asked my lady to pee on a stick. Real romantic, ain't I? She did and the lines showed we were on our way! Of course subsequent fears arose, occasionally wandering into thoughts of losing the baby. We didn't tell many people. I even adopted more of my wife's energy, preparing a space of comfort and ease.

Nine months later another home birth, this time a lot easier and based more on Mika's style. You can't call birth with no drugs "effortless," but it seemed to be basically that, with her screams and yells more "primal" and intuitive than cries for help. And…drum roll…it's a GIRL. It took decades, but my girl got her Chloe!! We have a daughter. She is beautiful, and looks just like her mommy. Still getting used to opening a diaper and seeing the "package missing." It almost startles me…

It cracks me up that I am known in comedy as "The Lovemaster," a character who is a sex-obsessed, cocky, confident guy, whose deep voice and talk of his large member attempts to sway the ladies into a bed where, "I'll love you so good, your SISTER's toes will curl, baby. I got thrown off a nude beach…for being over the LEGAL LIMIT. You'll be begging like PBS on a pledge drive."

Now I've somehow become the Love MASTER, assisting people into finding paramours and intimacy. I dig the moniker a lot more than the guy who wants to get laid!

You are my ninth fix-up that will result in marriage. Obviously we did not begin our exchanges with any clue this would transpire. Hell, I just thought I'd be able to assist you in bringing about a better situation with Matt. Had no clue you'd be marrying my kindergarten buddy! By the way, FYI, he's a cot hog, so get a big mattress.

I think all good results are born out of strong intentions of integrity. My desire all along, since I was little, is to make others happy. Even if it is as simple as gathering people for a party or get-together, my insides vibrate when I know I assisted a "healing" of sorts. Togetherness is such a pleasurable experience. Shared joy is putting extra sauce on the cheesesteak. Either that, or I'm just afraid of being alone! No wonder my best meditating is when someone is nearby. The perfect solo internal adventure takes place when someone is vacuuming in the other room.

I know you like to peek back at our little grace book, especially if a spiritual boost is needed. I too need to return to that space of grace and when I read some of our entries, it brings me back to where I need to be. Usually the best time to review is when Debby and I are going at it. Yes, can you believe that after almost ten years of separation, we still fight? Leah, I'm both shocked that the pattern still continues, and ashamed at my part in bringing it about. Hey, I just remembered one of the conclusions – I AM ONE HUNDRED PERCENT RESPONSIBLE FOR WHAT HAPPENS. It's my script and apparently I refuse to replace my villain. This calls for a serious re-write.

As I ponder this further; can you truly pen a life story without conflict? Hmmm. Will have to evaluate this one. I will say however, that despite Debby constantly threatening us and being typically non-compliant and unreasonable, this life o mine is pretty damn terrific. Makes me wonder if I hold onto her and our dynamic because I'm afraid of the even more enormous potential that exists. Hmmm (number 2). If indeed there was a true letting go of being "right," instead of expecting her to stop trying to always be right, would I feel completely fulfilled? Is writing this my inspiration to "heal thyself," and return to the guy whose purpose is absolute soul magnificence? Hmmm (number 3).

Leah, to be honest, I'm doing the old Shoe thing right this moment, up in the middle of the night, filled with anxiety over recent dealings with Debby. At no time in my life have things been more promising and exciting, yet here I am pulling focus by going at it with her in more ugly email exchanges. Also, the dialogue in my head is back – I'm actually believing that somehow my clever words will change her mind and hence her actions. Little ole hopeful Craigy is back in that place he was when he had faith his mommy would finally be loving and pay attention to a boy lost in a yearning that would never reveal itself. "Why can't my mother be NORMAL?" I would repeat to myself, as she had just pulled another self-absorbed display of, "I never wanted a boy." Or, "I see your father in you." I mentioned before about how I make cake out of crumbs but now realize I need to amend that analogy. Dealing with my mom, sister and Debby is like building a snowman close to the equator. In my mind there is an artistic design; with a top hat, corn cob pipe and button nose, just as the storybooks say it should be. But my dreams melt away the second the reality sets in that in these conditions, my visions are an illusion that will never become a reality. Maybe we can import some snow so I can have immediate joy, yet the idea is quickly turned to mush when the temperature of their untreated rage heats up.

It's the age-old question: Are they crazy by staying in the same behavioral pattern for a lifetime, or am I nuts to think they will someday understand it will not lead to happiness?

Probably both. Yes, I am a whack job.

Dear Whack Job, I have one word for you – SURRENDER. Time to raise the white flag of seeking truth for others. If they want to live in a pathology of lies and mistruths, they do so at their own peril. Just don't make it to your demise, Mr. Shoe. Every time you engage with them, you lose. This is their battleground, not yours, and if you think you can win, then you are truly out of your mind. They know no better, and quite naturally act in a manner that is comfortable to them. They do not want to live on a higher plain, so why do you try to convince them to join you on your road to inner Shangri-La? You can ask the Wicked Witch all day, every day, to follow the Yellow Brick Road but she has no interest in leaving the comfort of her castle. She holds dominion over her subjects, bathing in the darkness of lack and limitation. It is there she has power over her emotional hostages. It is in her confines where she can control others and have them believe the spin that a life on their own would lead to a sorry demise. Fear rules the day – through intimidation, guilt and threat. Flying monkeys surround them, coming to the belief that Her Highness's pat on the back for doing her bidding, will suffice in giving all the love available. For you, my dear, straight, male Dorothy, home is truly where the heart is. To deny the truth of what is, denies you of what could be. Live in the POSSIBLE and the "normal" you've dreamed of will be yours to enjoy!

A DEDICATION

Tough to find funny right now. Remember I wrote about my childhood friend with lung cancer, Rob Horner? He is now on full life support. It's really difficult to keep my mind focused when he clings to life. Especially hard in MY business! Even if I think of something funny to say, I ponder whether it's appropriate right now.

Known him since we were in second grade. Always a winner and resilient, which is why it is hard to think he won't somehow pull through. For many years, I organized getaway guy trips for a large group of childhood classmates and he has gone on every one, his pleasant spirit a key to our core. And boy, do we LAUGH. Sharing joy is the essential ingredient to our bond. To think we may have communed in levity for the last time makes me incredibly sad, somewhat paralyzed, as I keep thinking about him struggling for breath. So often we cried laughing, now I'm crying with the thought of not being able to do it in the same way again.

Right before he went into the hospital, he sent us (and a large group of his friends and family) a spiritual book called, *The Energy Bus.* The personal note enclosed ended with him letting me know he'd be at my comedy show outside Philly: "Love Ya. See you in Sellersville, Shoe."

I will be at the theatre at the end of this month. To think he won't be in that audience simply crushes me. No matter if he passes today, next week, or even pulls a miracle and lives to 100, he will always remind me that committed friendship, love and laughter are most important. Our memories are brimming with all that and then some. None of our stories and recollections includes money or acquisition but plenty of free silly. Sure, I might be the guy who supplies a few more of the jokes for our old gang, but if not for the connection with people like my dear friend, the humor would be meaningless. Laughter is heartful communication. It's opening to what is good, and my friend is one good man. Regarding Debby, or any other person whom I deem to be an adversary, I'm honoring Rob and putting out to the universe a commitment to kindness, generosity, good attitude and moral principle. Create memories like that and no matter how long we're here, you manifest a beautiful ride!

My sadness takes a pause as I reflect back on a story he & I share...

When we were 22, I took him on a Bahamas Windjammer Cruise I won in a talent contest. We got hammered drunk after he and I won another contest on board the ship, with Rob being dressed and performing as my ventriloquist dummy. It was REALLY funny, with Rob moving his mouth like a doll whenever I pressed on his back. Our prize was unlimited booze, and we imbibed with abandon. We went to sleep – he in the bottom bunk, me up top. Woke up the next morn, notice vomit covering the entire cabin floor. I say, "Rob, What the hell did you DO?! You gotta clean that up, buddy!" He looks at me like I'm nuts and insists it was ME who barfed on our floor! We shared cleanup duty, the entire time trying to prove the other to be the culprit. "Let me smell your breath." "This is some fucked up way to get me to help you clean up your puke."

Decades later, I never let up leaning on him to tell the truth, swearing it wasn't me, and I've always asked we keep an agreement we would confess on our deathbed. I know he would laugh right now if someone could get the message to him that, even with him in a coma, Shoe wants to know, "Was it YOU?"

I realize that even though I lived with him, played with him, traveled with him and even started an entrepreneurial business with Rob, we never had a cross word with one another in over 40 years of friendship. When Debby began to bring the false allegations a while back, Rob immediately sent a character letter to the evaluator on my behalf, spelling out the man I am from his eyes, not the predator Debby tries to convince all that I am. I just pulled out a copy of that letter and it moved me to both a bad memory of where I was at that time, and a beautiful feeling of someone taking the time to support me.

Every year or so, when I organize getaway weekends with guys from our old neighborhood, Rob is first in line to sign up, knowing how these times shared with people you love, leave an indelible mark on our souls. Or sometimes, a memory we'd like to forget! Ha. When he was diagnosed with lung cancer (non-smoker), we all knew if it was to be defeated, our friend was the one to do so, and he would do so with levity and purpose. Although I live 3000 miles away, the distance means nothing when it comes to nurturing friendship. Somehow, on the last guy trip I organized several months ago, an instinct made me think it might be his last. All our boys were laughing at goof-ass buddy, Shoe, wearing shorts to a fancy restaurant and having to go to a locker and borrow clothes the establishment has for dudes like me. We all howled that weekend.

[ONE DAY LATER]

On page 27 of *The Energy Bus,* which Rob sent days ago, there is a box that stands out in the middle, with a sentence about dying at 9am on a Monday. Today, on this Monday morning in February, Rob Horner passed away at 9 o'clock.

Even in death the guy got it right.

Leah, you might be happy to know that in losing his courageous battle, he caused something that I stated long ago I had been avoiding. I mentioned a few times to you that I did not have the ability to truly cry, fearing I would not stop. Well, this time the faucet was opened and out came a river. It brought me (literally) to my knees. He left too soon, but leaves us with memories of integrity, kindness and good spirit we will never forget. Rob & I dug our laughter bond. He even had me do standup comedy at his wedding, which I know he regretted! Comedy bits about "teenage erections" are not material for old aunts and uncles. LOL.

I won't be seeing him when I play Philly in a few weeks but the seats he purchased will remain empty and the laughs we have will be in his memory. LOVE YOU, ROB! And miss you already...

As my friends and I talk of our buddy Rob's legacy, it got me to thinking: Is it really the good dying young, or is it the reflection of our elevated self that comes more into focus? Is the "good" the person one desires to be?

Rob had a consistent way of being throughout his life: He was balanced, peaceful, athletic, bright, kind, stable and courageous. He shined with integrity and had an essence of positive flow. He thrived in possibility. However, no person can be all these things at all times. Even though he has been known in our neck of the woods as the handsome & rich guy who had it all, there were parts of him that he felt needed to be enriched or improved.

In the last 8 years or so, he and I began to have deeper conversations, extending well beyond our silliness or typical, "How's your family" fare. I mean, here's a guy I thought had it all, still wanting more fulfillment, love and higher consciousness. I used to visit his house growing up, wondering what it would be like to be so rich and lucky, and have great looks too. Yet here is that fortunate one, telling me how he too searches for more inner magnificence, not outward displays of the perception of it.

Yes, a good man died young yesterday but his greatness encourages me to extend beyond my comfort zone, centering each day in how I can make a positive mark on the world. Just 2 weeks ago, he Fed Exed a book to many of us that is about "fueling up" with positive energy. That's my pal, nudging us to live on with purpose.

I'm not sure if my old buddy engineered this from the beyond, but a miracle took place yesterday. People throw the miracle word around often, and usually attribute it to a paralyzed man being touched by a preacher and suddenly can walk.

It's certainly not to those proportions, but I was frozen regarding my sister Lizzy, and saw no possible way it could improve, yet something happened yesterday that has me dancing on air.

I held thought that I had exhausted every conceivable method of healing in the case with my mom and sister. I arrived to the place where I "let go" with my only sibling (from the same parents, that is). I stopped emailing requests to process with a professional and went into acceptance mode, figuring she simply will never "get it." I keep trying the emails with our mother, but concluded that I can drop the little Craigy fixer bit with Lizzy.

She was also close with Rob and had similar feelings as I held about his character. Who knows if he inspired this, but here is what happened…

I was on a radio show in Austin when I see her name on my phone, calling me first thing in the morning. Then she followed with a text. My first reaction was that she was telling me our mom died, and I continued the show holding that thought. Knowing Lizzy, or at least THINKING I knew her, I figured her agenda was not aligned with mine. We have not spoken in five years, and the responses to my emails and requests to meet on neutral ground have been refuted over and over again.

Of course I have similar judgment and feeling about her, being too eerily similar to my ex and mom.

No need for details, but she called to let me know she missed me. I could hear in her tone on the voicemail a noticeable shift. I called her and left my own tone. It was one of levity and no heaviness. We have an old way of speaking to ne another, a private joke, and I went right to it, merely saying: "Yyyyyyyyyyyyyyyyyyyyyyyyyyyooooooooooooooooooooooo…"

Fortunately and magically I was off of work and on the road in a hotel room and had zero distractions, giving full attention to a long needed conversation. We proclaimed right away that our intent was agreed upon, that we will work through the crap and move onto a space of love and support.

As in most disagreements, we share so much of the same traits. It is laughable. As much as we enjoy our commonalities, it seems there are ugly ones that hit some sour notes. But this conversation was different.

CRAIG SHOEMAKER

It was historical. We will both recall it with such fondness for the rest of our lives.

It began with catching up etc., as well as a bit of identifying some issues. The big deal for these two stuck ones – we made it through! EIGHT STRAIGHT HOURS, talking and talking on the phone. If we were younger, we never could have done it, because I don't think even our kids could text for THAT long! Haha.

We made it through. We had a wide assortment of topics, ranging from our children, to careers and doses of childhood recollections. However, the best part for me was trudging past a fight. Yes, it was frightening, both resorting to old tactics, pointing the finger to the other as the one who "enjoys" battling, all the while self proclaiming we don't like spats and try to avoid them. Funny, because at one point she says, "BREATHE, Craig!" I heard it as a command fired back, "YOU breathe!"

I am that, I am.

I am grinning ear to ear as I write this, since I have a newfound freedom and confidence moving forward with my little sis. We committed to making this work and not running away, even making an appointment with a professional. The best part for me, Lizzy truly acknowledged what I was saying and heard an alternative perspective. Seemingly for the first time in our lives, she seemed to be lighter and more accountable. It felt amazing to hear her say how much pain I must be feeling when both mom and sister "took Debby's side."

Contrary to what I had assessed about her, she went past self and humbly discussed solution. Pretty cool stuff. And to top the weird, out of nowhere hours of healing, she puts the TV on in the background and up pops my SHOWTIME special!! Whoa. WTF?? She giggles and turns up the volume. I had written a while ago that I wished my mother and sister expressed a little pride towards me. It turns out she had indeed seen my special a year ago, and minutes before she turned on her television, told me how amazing she thought it was. Then, boom, it is on in her living room, serving as background vocals to a new hit song.

At the end, which we thought was about 37 "I have to go to sleep(s)" ago, we talked about our mom. It helped immensely. It actually inspires me to approach mom in another way, and do so with a big load of acceptance of who she is, and that she will not budge from her positions. Yes, it is about what I can do to forgive, not what I expect from her.

A gigantic transformation of energy took place. I'm on the bus and allowing for an even better destination, leaving much of the driving to Big

Goodness. And I think the co pilot on this one was my old friend, who attempted to mend my family while on earth, and now perhaps smiling wide from spirit world.

I miss you, Rob, but I'm catching what you left us: No matter what life dishes out, find a way to manage through with positivity, dignity, character and laughter. And one thing our gang learned on our trips: If it rains on your outdoor plans...go bowling.

CRAIG SHOEMAKER

Craig Shoemaker has a Doctorate in Humane Letters from California University of Pennsylvania and has studied at The Agape Spiritual Center and Institute in Los Angeles, where he met his wife, Mika. As a comedian, he is best known for his character The Love Master and he has won numerous awards, including Comedian of the Year at the American Comedy Awards on ABC and two NATAS Emmys. His first Comedy Central Show was voted by viewers as one of the Top Twenty specials of all time and his ninety-minute special Daditude premiered on Showtime in 2013. He hosts a weekly podcast/webcast at craigshoemaker.com about combining personal wellness and healing laughter.